"I Am Very Spontaneous,"

she announced stiffly, and he laughed.

"Don't be ridiculous. You haven't done one spontaneous thing since you got here."

"Neither have you," Emily countered. "In fact, you've been quite calculating."

Spencer frowned, considering. Suddenly he leaned over and kissed her. His lips were warm and insistent, and they tasted like sweet wine. "Was that spontaneous enough for you?"

"I—" she choked.

"Or this?" He kissed her again.

"That was completely uncalled for!" Emily said tersely. "This was supposed to be a job interview!"

"Is that what you're worried about?" Spencer smiled. "Well, don't. You're already hired."

DIANA MORGAN
lives in a romantic area called Park Slope, which is full of Victorian townhouses. She is also a literary agent in New York, and the proud parent of a beautiful baby girl named Elizabeth.

Dear Reader:

In the three years since Silhouette Books began publishing with Silhouette Romances we've seen many new developments: American settings and heroines, stronger, more independent characters, longer, more sensual stories and some exciting new authors who have appeared on the scene.

It was during this first year that many of you discovered new favorites including Dixie Browning, Nora Roberts, Brooke Hastings and many others. These authors have continued to write new and exciting stories, whether they are for Silhouette Romance, Silhouette Special Edition, Silhouette Desire or for Silhouette Intimate Moments.

Now you have an opportunity to buy those first books by some of your favorite authors. This month, be sure to look for the "Springtime is Romance time" display wherever you buy books.

Karen Solem
Editor-in-Chief
Silhouette Books

DIANA MORGAN
Behind Closed Doors

Silhouette Romance

Published by Silhouette Books New York

America's Publisher of Contemporary Romance

SILHOUETTE BOOKS, a Division of Simon & Schuster, Inc.
1230 Avenue of the Americas, New York, N.Y. 10020

ISBN: 0-671-57293-8

First Silhouette Books printing May, 1984

10 9 8 7 6 5 4 3 2 1

To Uncle Wally
and the Secret Society of
Schwartzes

1134/445/FII FPJ
FENTON INTERNATIONAL INDUSTRIES
MESSAGE FROM CENTRAL COMPUTER FILES {NEW CODE: ESMERELDA}
TO: J.P. FENTON, PRESIDENT

UNDERSTAND REQUEST FOR EMPLOYEE DATA CLASSIFICATION

SUBJECT: EMILY MOREAU
AGE: 24
PHYSICAL: RED HAIR, GREEN EYES, 5'-4", 110 LBS.
JOB TITLE: COMPUTER PROGRAMMER
TIME WITH FENTONS: 3 YEARS, 4 MONTHS, 12 DAYS
EDUCATION: PRINCETON UNIVERSITY; B.S., M.S.
    COMPUTER SCIENCE
PRIOR EMPLOYMENT: TAP DANCER, UNCLE ERNIE'S
    CHILDREN'S HOUR
FENTON EMPLOYMENT RECORD: PROMOTED 1 YEAR, HEAD OF
    SOFTWARE DIVISION, WINNER OF FENTON ANNUAL
    COMPUTER PROGRAMMER AWARD
EMPLOYEE STATUS: TERMINATED; CONDOLENCE FLOWERS SENT

SUBJECT: SPENCER MCINTYRE
AGE: 31
PHYSICAL: BROWN HAIR, BLUE EYES, 5'-11", 160 LBS.
JOB TITLE: PRESIDENT OF MCINTYRE, INC., COMPUTER
    CONSULTING COMPANY
EDUCATION: HARVARD UNIVERSITY; B.S., M.S.
    COMPUTER SCIENCE
PRIOR EMPLOYMENT: SELF EMPLOYED FOR PAST 6 YEARS
FENTON EMPLOYMENT RECORD: HIRED TO ANALYZE FEASIBILITY
    OF COMPUTER SYSTEM. RECOMMENDED 75% OF COMPUTER
    EMPLOYEES TERMINATE IMMEDIATELY: ACCEPTED
QUOTE WALTER DRYSDALE N.Y. TIMES: ''A VERITABLE 20TH
    CENTURY GENIUS''
FENTON STATUS: ON RETAINER INDEFINITELY

LOVE,
ESMERELDA

P.S. TAKE THE REST OF THE DAY OFF, BOSS. YOU SEEM TENSE.

1134/445/FII FPJ

Chapter One

"Spooky, isn't it?" the man asked conversationally, balancing his chair on its two back legs against the wall. He propped his feet up on the computer terminal in front of him, watching her with a leisurely attitude. "Almost like a morgue."

Emily frowned, reluctant to admit that she agreed.

His candid gaze raked over her trim figure as if he had nothing better to do and was examining her merely for his own amusement. It was impossible to ignore him; they were quite alone in the terminal room, surrounded by the weight of the unaccustomed silence. Usually, every seat at every terminal was occupied on a Friday afternoon as the programmers rushed to complete the new sets of commands for the main computer, sitting in state three floors below. But that day everything was different. After she let the computer digest the last bits of information she would ever feed it, she would walk out the door forever. In the space of three short weeks, all of her colleagues had been fired. She would be the last to go.

The man looked at her quizzically, waiting for an answer to his question.

"Who are you?" she asked point-blank, although she was almost certain that she already knew.

"The grim reaper." He didn't smile, and neither did

she. "I'm the reason this branch of the company will no longer exist after five o'clock today."

She nodded stonily. "That's what I thought, Mr. McIntyre."

"At your service, Ms. Moreau," he answered, nodding back pleasantly.

"You know who I am?" Emily was disconcerted.

His glance swept ironically over the empty room. The computers sat dully, row upon row, their faces looking more like epitaphs than screens. The room had once been a busy place, bustling with activity, but now the ghosts of her colleagues seemed to hover over the vacant chairs. The fluorescent lighting was a poor excuse for the lack of any windows, and the only sound came from the monotonous hum of cool air as it circulated through the vents in the ceiling. "Of course I know who you are," he responded calmly. "Process of elimination. You were chosen to be the last to go."

"By you, Mr. McIntyre," she retorted. "It's a dubious honor."

She maintained her composure as she went back to her keyboard, but inside she was seething. After three years of loyal service to Fenton International Industries, she'd been unceremoniously booted out. And all because of Spencer McIntyre, who'd been contracted as a consultant by the company. His final analysis had been to fire seventy-five percent of all programmers, and the recommendation had been carried out without delay.

She could feel him watching her but forced herself to keep on working. His chair bumped the wall occasionally as he tilted it to and fro, and the sounds it made seemed deliberately calculated to annoy her. Her father had taught her to listen to the sounds people made in order to know what they were thinking. The methodical bump of McIntyre's chair clearly defined his attitude; he was all smugness.

"You know, Emily," he said after a while, his tone confirming her analysis. "I can't figure you people out. You all get fired. Dropped like hot potatoes after three faithful years. And yet you stay here dutifully, working until the bitter end. Doesn't it bother you? Don't you want to just get up and leave?"

It was a loaded question, and she didn't answer it. She lined up the last part of the last program on the screen, watching as the numbers appeared. The greenish glow cast a strange light on her face, giving her an unearthly look.

"You must be a saint," he said, answering his own question. "That's it. And that green light on your hair is a halo." Again, she held her tongue, wondering in irritation just when he was going to stop. His gaze wandered to the neat coil of hair on top of her head. "Look at all that gorgeous auburn hair," he remarked. "So tightly bundled up in a knot. You ought to let it down, let it flow over your shoulders. That's your problem," he continued, adding to her annoyance. "You're too uptight. Too regimented."

He waited for her to react, but she refused to rise to the bait. Her eyes were still glued to the screen. At that moment, her last program was going out to every Fenton terminal all over the world. Somewhere in Japan, a man was sitting at a terminal exactly like hers, watching her program appear as she dictated the final commands for the main computer to absorb into its data bank. She had the sudden urge to type in a final farewell to the people who had been lucky enough to survive the massacre.

GOOD-BYE, ALL YOU SURVIVORS, she typed in. ALL MY LOVE, EMILY MOREAU. She pressed the return key to enter the final message, but to her dismay, the computer spit it back.

ILLOGICAL, it spewed across the top line of the screen. DOES NOT COMPUTE.

"You insensitive hunk of metal!" she cried, banging her fist down on the desk.

"Take it easy," Spencer admonished with mock gravity from in back of her. "You wouldn't want to hurt the computer's feelings, would you? After all, she's doing one heck of a job, wouldn't you say?"

"Too good a job," she answered bitterly. "She just replaced seventy-five percent of the computer staff." Emily spun around in her swivel chair and stopped the motion by lodging her feet firmly on the floor. "What makes you think the computer is a 'she,' anyway?"

"Because," he explained, the smugness returning, "computers, like women, are very touchy. They have to be handled with tender loving care or they become very disagreeable."

"What an enlightened viewpoint," she returned dryly.

Spencer smiled, and she decided to ignore him once again. She turned around in her chair to face the terminal, determined to avoid further conversation with him. The last person she wanted to spend her last few minutes with on the job was the man who had recommended that she and hundreds of others be fired. She knew of his reputation but had dismissed it as the result of rumors and exaggeration. No one could possibly live up to such an outlandish reputation.

She'd been told that he was a nomad, a hired gun, so to speak. Anyone who had a problem with their computer that was too big or too confounding for their own personnel to handle would call on Spencer McIntyre.

If they could find him. He had no known address

except for a post-office box at Grand Central Station, and he lived in hotel rooms, always on the move. She'd heard other rumors about him. He had allegedly saved millions of dollars for a handful of companies during the past few years.

Her curiosity got the better of her despite her resolve. "I heard you made quite a splash at your last assignment," she remarked without looking around.

Somehow she knew that he was smiling broadly. A quick glance revealed that she was right. "I suppose you could say that," he answered, falsely modest. "They wanted to improve public relations within the ranks, so I hooked up the computer to the Telex system and ordered it to send candygrams to all the employees on their birthdays."

She almost missed a beat, but she forced her fingers to continue their work. Her back became rigid, however, and she knew it was easy for him to detect her discomfort.

"What's the matter, Emily?" he asked softly.

She spun around suddenly and faced him. "It's all a game to you, isn't it? You don't care that you affect the lives of people who need their jobs. Candygrams!" She shook her head. "What next?" she finished rhetorically.

For the first time, he seemed to take her seriously. "No," he said, frowning, "that's not true. It's just that I like to be in control of things, and computers help me out."

She didn't answer, and he got up and stood behind her, his nearness making her tingle inexplicably. They both stared at the screen where the words DOES NOT COMPUTE still glowed greenly. He reached around her with both arms and typed in a response to that: DOES NOT FEEL.

The computer's response was inevitable; the words

DOES NOT COMPUTE immediately returned, silently stubborn.

"A metallic monster," he announced quietly. "A marvel of electronic machinery that thinks but does not feel."

"I thought you said it was a woman," she countered unwillingly, wondering why she was getting involved in the conversation at all. "You called it a 'she.'"

"An electronic mistress, then," he acknowledged. "Heartless, cold, calculating . . ." He smiled humorlessly. "An evil necessity of the modern age."

He was still leaning over her, his arms pinning her arms to her sides. She tried delicately to dislodge his hold, but he was oblivious, staring intently at the screen. "This 'evil necessity' has made you a millionaire," she said sharply, to distract his attention. She felt him stiffen slightly, and she continued in a rush. "You come in here to do some simple feasibility studies on this computer, and three weeks later seventy-five percent of our staff is fired. What feelings do *you* have for them?"

"I never recommended that anyone be fired." He sounded genuinely surprised, and her temper flared. But to her relief, he stood up suddenly, backing away and sitting back down in his chair. "You know, Emily, you jump to conclusions. Sometimes I think this computer is smarter than you are."

Her green eyes blazed. "Don't be ridiculous," she said hotly. "You're as cold and heartless as any computer, and you know it. If you didn't recommend all those terminations, then who did—Mr. Fenton?"

To her dismay, he stood up and came behind her again, reaching around her slim frame to type something into the computer. She could sense the anger in him, as if he was annoyed at her lack of logic. Or lack of control over the computer. That was the one thing he had said he liked about computers—the control they gave him. She read his impatience from the quick, sharp intake of breath, and she sat stiffly as he rapidly entered a request.

LIST COMPUTER PERSONNEL PRIOR TO TERMINATION ORDER # 287-SDF.

Instantly, the screen was alive with a running list of names, flying by in alphabetical order. Emily recognized many of them as friends who were no longer employed by Fenton. She stared for a moment, trying to absorb the immensity of it, but by the time it got to the G's, she was dizzy.

Spencer's finger brought the parade to a sudden stop, and with one quick move, the screen was once again blank.

CONCLUDE FEASIBILITY STUDY ON COMPUTER PERSONNEL, he typed in, and again the computer obediently furnished the information.

EMPLOYEE NECESSITY STUDY # 287-SDF: 25% EFFICIENCY, it answered promptly.

"I was asked to update this computer and bring it up to maximum efficiency," Spencer explained. "I found that it could actually do most of its own work—seventy-five percent, to be exact. This meant that seventy-five percent of the computer personnel could be used more advantageously, perhaps transferred to some other area. But J. P. Fenton doesn't listen to the plain advice of a mere human being, not when he has a multimillion-dollar computer to tell him what to do." He broke away from her, chuckling quietly to himself. "I recommended that he upgrade the entire system, using all of the seventy-five percent in question. But I was outrecommended."

"By whom?" she demanded, twisting around in her chair to face him.

An odd mixture of impatience and sympathy seemed

to pass across his face. Then he came behind her again and tersely typed in another command. SUMMARIZE EMPLOYEE EFFICIENCY STUDY # 287-SDF.

The answer flashed immediately: 25% EFFICIENT, it stated once again.

Spencer typed another order. CONCLUDE RECOMMENDATION FOR EMPLOYEE EFFICIENCY STUDY # 287-SDF.

As Emily watched speechlessly, the screen lit up with the mechanical response. TERMINATE 75% COMPUTER PERSONNEL.

Spencer began to chuckle again, this time with a liberal amount of irony. "Congratulations, Emily," he said. "You just programmed yourself right out of a job."

She could think of absolutely nothing to say.

"And here you sit," he continued, "loyal to the end. Utterly rank and file," he added. "Just like the army." He shook his head again, gave her a wry smile, and strode out the door, leaving her alone in the empty room.

She stared at the doorway for a moment, looking after him as his footsteps receded down the corridor. Then all was silent again, and she turned reluctantly back to the computer screen that sat waiting for her. Its blank glow seemed to be mocking her, and she repeated his last words over and over in her mind. He was right. Fired by a computer! It was that simple.

She gazed at the mechanical monster that had usurped her position with a growing sense of animosity. As McIntyre's simple, infuriating logic danced around mercilessly in her mind, her fingers danced restlessly over the keys, and a highly dissatisfied expression spread across her face. Before she had any idea why she did it, she typed a rhetorical question that appeared immediately on the screen.

WHY?

There were a few seconds of potent silence, during which she knew the electronic brain was searching for the answer. Finally, to her amusement, it came back with a question of its own. WHY WHAT? it asked simply.

Emily smiled, wondering if she should continue the absurd conversation. The words stood out on the screen, staring at her as she contemplated her next move.

WHY WAS I FIRED?

The machine digested that one, and presently it supplied a response:

```
EMPLOYEE #124-40-7435 EMILY MOREAU
REASONS FOR TERMINATION:
PROJECT COMPLETED
PROGRAM SELF-SUFFICIENT
EMPLOYEE NO LONGER REQUIRED
```

DROP DEAD, Emily printed, letting her anger get the best of her.

But the computer could only respond in the mechanical language it had been taught. MUST REPHRASE. CANNOT COMPUTE.

"You cold-blooded contraption," she muttered aloud. "Someone ought to teach you some compassion. Not to mention some manners." Her fingers toyed with the keys as a bittersweet smile spread over her face. "In fact, a little politeness would do you a world of good."

The thought was so outlandish that her despondency vanished, replaced at once by amusement. If only someone could teach such things to a computer, she thought. It was probably possible, but no one had ever tried it.

She looked at the huge machine with irritation. Then

she laughed. "Sure why not? It's worth a try." After all, she reasoned, if computers could send candy to employees on their birthdays, then surely they could learn other amenities as well. All at once her mind seemed to snap into action as the various permutations entered her brain. A little manipulation in the software here, add another program there . . . She smiled half jokingly to herself and said with a nod, "Yes, it's quite possible, after all."

She looked up at the clock to make sure she had enough time. Why not try it? She had nothing better to do on that dismal evening. Why not spend the time creating a program to soften the metal heart of a computer. What a crazy way to end her career at Fenton!

Standing up, she went over to the shelf in the corner and lightly drew a blank tape from the files and threaded it into the machine. Then she was off and running down the hall to the company library, where she began examining the books she would need. "I'll give this computer some feelings that will make it cry real tears," she announced. Quickly scanning the titles, she chose *Emily Post's Book of Etiquette* and, after a moment's hesitation, *The Dictionary of Rhymes* and *Mother Goose*.

Back at her terminal, she stacked the books next to her and thought for a few minutes before beginning.

"We'll start by giving you a name." E-S-M-E-R-E-L-D-A, she typed out, and watched as the spool of tape spun a half a turn, absorbing the new information.

"Just the beginning," she said. She opened the first book and went to work feeding it into the tape. The keys flew under her deft fingers, each new bit of information driving her to add even more.

"Okay, Mr. Spencer McIntyre," she said softly as

she forged ahead. "I'm going to create a Frankenstein of my own. Only the brain I transplant into the computer's head will be good, not evil."

She went through all the fine points of Emily Post, and when that was finished, she opened the *Dictionary of Rhymes* and set up a system that would enable the computer to randomly rhyme anything it wanted to say. "Four stanzas, double rhymes. That should do the trick." It was so simple that she wondered why no one had ever done it before. In no time at all, she had taught the computer to match all phonetic word endings, and Esmerelda was on her way to becoming an instant poet. After she programmed in the short verses, Esmerelda was capable of writing a typical greeting card for any occasion.

Emily continued her work as the time flew by. She became so involved that she didn't bother to look up at the clock as she drove on and on, working permutation against permutation. The tape on the spool moved steadily, absorbing bit by bit, until at last, four more books and several hours later, she fell back in her chair, exhausted. When she looked up, she could see that the spool on the computer had been filled.

Reluctantly, she withdrew it from the machine and held it in her hand the way a bounty hunter would hold an empty jewel case. She wondered what would happen if she actually ran the tape through the computer. No doubt it would knock Fenton International Industries on its ear. The notion was certainly tempting.

She went back to her seat by the terminal, still clutching the new software package she had just created. Turning it over in her hands, she examined it as if it were a strip of celluloid imprinted with the frames of a movie. It would be so easy to open up the computer for input and feed it the tape of new instructions. The personality of a new machine would then spring to life.

"What a bang-up way to leave the company," she murmured, her eyes twinkling for a second. She imagined old man Fenton walking into his office and discovering Esmerelda, the poet computer, controlling his billion-dollar corporation. The idea was priceless. She tossed the spool into the air a few times, catching it with a little giggle. But her celebration was short-lived as she came to her senses and caught the tape neatly, enclosing it safely in her fist.

Take it easy, Emily. It was her father's influence speaking from within her, loud and clear. Your job here is finished, and you did the best you could. Now it's time to leave—and leave everything the way you found it. You can take pride in a job that is completed and well done.

As she sat there, tape in hand, she realized she'd never had any intention of running such a program through the computer. Good judgment had overruled. It was time to pack up and go home. Her days at Fenton were now over.

Shaking her head ruefully at the way she had spent the last few hours, she picked the tape up in her hand and examined it wistfully one more time. Then, in a single overhand motion, she tossed it in the direction of the wastebasket, hearing the clink of metal against metal as it landed.

"That's the best place for it," she concluded. "Unfortunately."

Her footsteps echoed hollowly as she left the building. "He was right," she muttered to herself as she swung through the door. "I'm hopelessly rank and file. Just as computerized as a computer." She sighed. "It's the old army brat in me, I guess."

Florence Luchek, the cleaning woman, entered the terminal room at eleven P.M. that same night, humming tunelessly to herself. "'Just one of those things, just one of those crazy things' . . ." She began to empty trash cans, dumping their contents into the large canvas bin that sat on four wheels. Suddenly, her eye caught sight of the computer tape that sat on the floor next to one of the wastebaskets. She frowned, bending over with a grunt to pick it up. Was it meant to be thrown away? Or should she leave it where it was?

Better to be safe than sorry. She placed the tape on a shelf directly over the largest terminal and went back to work, pushing her cart out the door and down the hall. "'It was just one of those things . . .'"

Chapter Two

"How extensive is the damage?" Spencer McIntyre, his back to the twelve very nervous men who comprised the executive board of Fenton International Industries, gazed down at the view from the forty-second floor of the Fenton Building in downtown Manhattan. The Wall Street lunch crowd was just thinning out, and the men and women on the narrow sidewalks looked like ants as they scurried to and fro. From where Spencer stood, he could see all the way to the harbor, where the Statue of Liberty kept her vigilant watch.

"We believe it's worldwide, Mr. McIntyre," a dapper young man answered anxiously. His hands shook as he lit a cigarette, and the others shuffled uncomfortably. "According to our London and Tokyo offices, the problem has been traced right back here, to the main computer bank."

McIntyre listened patiently, turning around slowly to face his audience. Twelve earnest faces gazed at him in despair.

"Do you think you can help us?" It was Thompson, the youngest of the vice-presidents. He was immaculately groomed and dressed in a tailored three-piece suit, but his eyes darted fearfully around the room, flitting over the half-empty cups of coffee and the overflowing ashtrays.

The group was waiting hopefully for McIntyre's

reply, and he hid a smile as he looked at the elegantly attired men. They looked exactly like naughty school children waiting for the principal—or in this case, their president, J. P. Fenton—to bawl them out. But Spencer McIntyre didn't fear Fenton. In contrast to the executive board, he was dressed casually in tan corduroy pants and a burgundy sweater over a plaid shirt.

He drew his lean, tightly muscled body to its full height and ran a hand through his thick, slightly disheveled brown hair. From the rumors he had already heard, he knew that J. P. Fenton believed in cold-blooded expediency. Fenton employees were merely tools, to be used and discarded when they were no longer needed. Spencer grimaced, wondering how much patience Fenton would have if he knew that Spencer McIntyre, the top consultant he had called in to streamline his system, was stumped. For the first time in his quirky, brilliant career, Spencer didn't know if he could meet the challenge for which he was being royally paid. Whoever had mangled the computer had certainly done a masterful job.

The tall, plush chair at the head of the long conference table was empty, and Spencer sat down in it heavily. The men exchanged nervous glances, and Thompson coughed. "Uh—Mr. McIntyre? Perhaps you'd be more comfortable over here." He gestured to another seat, but Spencer waved him off, concentrating on his decision.

"How long has the computer been malfunctioning?" he asked, leaning back in the oversized chair and stretching his arms expansively over the sides.

"Since 9:27 A.M., eastern standard time," Thompson answered dutifully. Spencer nodded for the man to continue. "We heard it first from Geneva. They were just wrapping up for the day, when it seems the computer just—stopped. It—well, it—it—"

"It what?" Spencer prompted him.

Thompson took a deep breath. "It scolded them."

"Scolded them!" Spencer repeated, his decisive eyebrows arching sharply. His bold gray eyes scanned Thompson's face for a sign of levity, but the man was perfectly serious.

"Yes, sir. The computer refused to cooperate until the word 'please' was added to its vocabulary. So everyone started saying 'please,' and everything went fine until—" He was interrupted by the ringing of the telephone. It had been ringing continually all day long, and he grabbed it resignedly. "Yes?" His face turned crimson as he listened. "The computer did *what?*" A few seconds passed, and he hung up without another word. "That was Los Angeles," he announced. "The computer has just arranged for flowers to be sent to all the employees we let go in the last month—with condolences!" He turned to Spencer. "How on earth can a computer do that?"

The expert shrugged. "Your computer can do everything. It controls every facet of your company. Nothing goes on here that the computer doesn't either plan or record."

The oldest vice-president frowned. "Is that so? Sounds pretty excessive to me. Whose idea was that, anyway?"

"Mine," came a voice in the doorway, and they all turned to see J. P. Fenton standing there, an unpleasant scowl on his seamed face. "It was supposed to streamline procedure." The short but powerfully intimidating man walked into the room, his eyes focusing instantly on the newcomer. "You are . . . ?" he asked directly.

"Uh—Mr. Fenton, this is Spencer McIntyre," Thompson volunteered. "You brought him in as a consultant about a month ago."

Spencer nodded cordially as he reached for his

lighter and lit up his pipe. He didn't make a move to vacate Fenton's chair, and the president regarded him coolly.

"Now I remember you, McIntyre," he said. "You're a nomad. A gypsy. A troubleshooter who hops from place to place."

"That's right, Fenton," Spencer replied cheerfully. "And right now, you need this gypsy pretty badly."

"Then you can repair the damage?" Fenton asked, getting right down to business. Before Spencer could answer, the telephone rang, and Fenton picked it up, snarling, "What now?" His face grew tense as he listened, and after a moment, he said tersely, "I don't care what the damn thing calls itself. I want production up to par!" He slammed down the phone and looked angrily at the twelve men on his board. "The computer has gone completely berserk," he informed them. "It has announced that its name is Esmerelda, and it won't furnish any more information unless it is addressed politely—by name!"

A ripple of surprise and discomfort spread rapidly through the group, but Spencer looked down, his lips twitching in merriment. He would have to keep this job if only for the sheer entertainment of it. When he looked up, he saw all of them looking at him expectantly. "So what you have here," he concluded calmly, "is a runaway computer."

Fenton placed his palms flat on the table and leaned over heavily to look McIntyre squarely in the eye. "Can you fix it?"

Spencer ignored the intimidation and got up, ambling over to the window to look out. "I've handled worse," he stated briefly.

"But can you fix this?" Fenton demanded. This time his voice was edged with just the slightest touch of desperation, and Spencer began to smile.

"If I can't," he answered without turning around, "there's only one person who can."

Fenton's impatience rose swiftly. "And who is that?"

Spencer looked once more at the Statue of Liberty in the harbor and then turned around to face them all. "Whoever started the problem in the first place," he said. "Of course." His broad smile lit up the room.

The telephone was ringing insistently as Emily fumbled for the key to her apartment in Brooklyn Heights. A bouquet of slightly wilting flowers lay draped across the welcome mat, and she scooped it up as she hurried inside. She dropped her suitcase on the floor, threw the flowers on a table, and dashed over to the telephone.

"Hello?" she gasped, out of breath.

"Ms. Moreau?"

"Speaking," she answered crisply.

"I'm calling in regard to your last job," the man continued.

Her last job? No one knew about her departure from Fenton. What was this all about?

"Ms. Moreau? Are you there?"

"Yes," she replied coolly. "Who is this?"

"Have you found another job yet?" Whoever he was, he certainly didn't waste any time. The voice sounded fleetingly familiar, but she couldn't quite place it.

"A job?" She still hadn't caught her breath, but she thought fast. "As a matter of fact, I have," she lied. "I start tomorrow."

"Cancel that." It was nothing less than a command, and for a moment she found herself about to obey.

"Now wait just a minute," she protested. "Who *is* this?"

"Your new boss."

She blinked. "Well, I'm very sorry, but as I told you, I already have a new job." She paused. "How did you know I needed a job, anyway? I've only been available for a couple of weeks, and I've been gone most of that time."

She could almost hear him thinking on the other end, and he said abruptly, "Whatever they're paying you, I'll double it."

Emily stepped backward and plunked down in a chair.

"I tried to reach you last Friday, but there was no answer," he added.

"I was away for the last two weeks," she explained, wondering why she was getting into this conversation in the first place.

"Oh, no wonder," he said. "Well, I'm glad I finally got you this morning. This situation calls for desperate measures."

"What situation?" she frowned.

"I'll explain it to you over lunch."

"Lunch?"

"It's almost twelve now. Just jump into a cab and meet me at—"

"Hold it," she interrupted. "This is insane. I'm not going anywhere until you tell me what this is all about."

"Not now. I can't talk where I am right now. Just trust me, and I'll tell you all about it over lunch."

"But who *are* you?" she shouted.

"Spencer McIntyre," he answered impatiently, as if she should have known. She sat up with a jolt, reminded of the odd meeting they had had two weeks before. "Meet me at the Marrakesh Express," he was saying rapidly, "122½ West Broadway, at twelve-thirty. Now get going, and don't be late. Or you're fired," he added jovially as an afterthought.

Emily hurriedly wrote down everything he said, and they hung up. Then she dropped the pencil and let out a long breath. Spencer McIntyre! Why on earth would he want to see her now? She frowned, involuntarily remembering his keen gray eyes, which seemed to look right through her. He had a job for her? It didn't seem likely, but that was what he had said.

But one thing was indisputable. She was most definitely in need of a job. She stood up, her mind made up. If the mercurial McIntyre wanted to see her, she would go out of curiosity, if nothing else. And if he really had a job for her, she'd better look her best.

She had only a few minutes, so she changed quickly into her "interview outfit"—a conservative beige suit with a cream-colored blouse and matching beige shoes. There was no time to pin her long, auburn hair neatly on top of her head, so she hastily ran a brush through it and clasped it together at the nape of her neck, George Washington style. She glanced quickly in the mirror. She looked neat and presentable. Snatching her handbag from the closet, she ran outside to look for a taxi.

The day was unseasonably warm, and a gentle breeze blew in from the harbor. Emily could see the crown of the Statue of Liberty looming in the distance as she hailed a cab and stepped inside.

"Take me to 122½ West Broadway," she said to the driver.

The man turned all the way around and looked at her suspiciously. "Where? What kinda place is that?"

"It's a restaurant. Are you sure you can find it?"

He shrugged disdainfully and switched on the meter. "If it's there, I'll find it." The cab lurched forward, headed for Manhattan.

Twenty minutes later, after circling the same block three times, they pulled over to the curb. "Look, lady," the driver said. "There ain't no such place. I've had some crazy addresses, but this one takes the cake."

He pointed at the doorways. "There's 120, and there's 122 and 124. There's nothing in between."

Emily looked. He was right. She sat helplessly, wondering what to do, when she caught sight of a thin young man dressed all in black, carrying a large easel. He walked down a flight of steps that descended from the street and opened a red door marked 122½.

"There it is!" she exclaimed. The driver threw up his hands, shaking his head, and she paid him and jumped out of the cab.

She emerged into a strange neighborhood that seemed to be tucked between Soho and the World Trade Center. The narrow street was lined with warehouses on one side and tall, rickety townhouses on the other side. The zigzag of fire escapes crossed the buildings, and a few lines of laundry hung between the windows of adjacent apartments. A lone street vendor stood at the corner with a wagon of roasted chestnuts, and Emily hurried past him to the red door marked 122½.

She opened it cautiously and was immediately greeted by a rush of warm air and a tantalizing aroma. The sinuous strains of Middle Eastern music tinkled faintly in the background, and as she stepped inside, she saw that she was in a small, dark room. Lanterns decorated with elaborate mosaics and graceful Arabic letters seemed to be the only source of light. As her eyes adjusted, she realized with a start that the patrons lounged casually on the floor in small groups. The tables were small and round, built right into the floor, and there were soft, plush pillows scattered generously around them.

"Miss Moreau?" A dark, sleek man with a moustache came toward her with a smile. "I am Faisal, the owner of the Marrakesh Express. Mr. McIntyre is expecting you. Will you follow me, please?"

They stepped around a group that sat by the door, and she followed him through the room and through an archway that led to an even darker room. "I am happy to see that Mr. McIntyre has a guest," Faisal said conversationally.

"Why?"

"He always dines alone. This is the first time he has entertained anyone since he has been a customer here."

Emily said nothing but looked around curiously. She could see smaller cubicles tucked behind filmy curtains at the sides of the room, and a large, three-tiered fountain made of green and blue tiles created an ever-present sound of rushing water. She was just thinking that the entire effect was somewhat hypnotic when Faisal drew aside one of the curtains in back of her. She turned to see a man lounging leisurely on the floor. He was surrounded by a riotous display of multicolored pillows that were intricately embroidered in gold and silver thread.

She stared down at him awkwardly, and he returned the gaze with one of frank interest that seemed mingled with surprise.

"Is there something wrong?" she faltered.

"We meet again, Ms. Moreau," he beamed.

"Uh—yes. Are you sure you called the right person?" She was beginning to fidget.

"Of course." His keen gray eyes roamed over every inch of her, fairly radiating with intelligence. They were edged by tiny laugh lines that represented both experience and mirth. Once again, he seemed to look right through her effortlessly, summing up her every thought and calculating the results.

"Are we still on for lunch?" she asked finally.

"Oh, yes, yes," he said, gesturing at the pillows. "Just kick off your shoes and drop down."

She obeyed hesitantly, slipping off her pumps. After placing several pillows in a neat row, she sat down cautiously, trying hard to keep her skirt from crawling above her knees. He watched her performance, never taking his eyes from her, and she could see that he was enjoying himself.

"You know something?" he said. "I am seldom wrong, but I was wrong about you." He leaned forward boldly to study her further in the dim light, his foot moving in time to the rhythmic music that echoed softly around them.

She tried to stare back at him and couldn't. "Why do I get the feeling I'm being observed as if I were under a microscope?"

Spencer retreated immediately. "Sorry. It's just that I thought you'd still have a chip on your shoulder after losing your job."

"Oh, really?" She tried to frown at him disapprovingly but ended up squinting instead in the flickering shadows. "Well, I don't."

"I know," he said, beaming. "I can see that."

"And what do you see instead?" she persisted, unable to resist her own curiosity.

"I'm not sure," he mused. "But I think that behind that Mona Lisa smile, there's a pixie trying to get out." He nodded, pleased with his analysis. "You know something, Emily?" He stretched his long, lean legs out in front of him. "I have a feeling that you're going to be full of surprises. Am I right?"

The Mona Lisa smile remained, but the unconscious twinkle in her eyes vanished. The effect was a Cheshire cat grin that hung suspended, and he laughed delightedly.

"Do I amuse you that much?" she asked seriously.

Before he could answer, Faisal appeared through the curtain, turning to Emily with a small bow. "Would the lady care for a drink?"

"Yes," she replied quickly, thinking that she could certainly use one. "I'd like a white wine."

Faisal nodded and turned to leave, but Spencer stopped him. "And I'll have a dry martini," he announced.

The man turned back, surprise covering his face. "A martini, sir? But you never drink!"

"First time for everything," Spencer answered cheerfully. "Make it extra dry, with a twist."

"Coming right up." Faisal disappeared through the gauzy curtain, and they were left alone again. There was a pause, during which the music seemed to swell around them, and their shadows loomed in silhouette against the wall. Emily tucked the hem of her skirt over her knees and took a long breath. It would be best to take control of the situation before things got out of hand.

"I have one question for you," she stated with more firmness than she felt. "How did you find me?"

His eyes flashed with the trace of a smile, and she noted with some annoyance that he seemed to be just as comfortable as she was self-conscious. "Let's just say that a very friendly computer furnished me with your background." He leaned back coolly, folding his arms.

Emily shook her head. "I should have known. And what did it tell you about me?"

"Born Lake Charles, Louisiana," he rattled off calmly. "Skipped third grade. Winner of the bubble-blowing contest at—"

"Now wait a minute," she interrupted, sitting up in alarm. "Where did you find a computer that knew that?" She looked worriedly back at him. He didn't respond, merely giving her an engaging grin, and she gestured for him to continue. "Don't let me stop you," she said wryly. "What else do you know?"

"All the pertinent data." His smile became triumphant. "Except for one extremely vital fact that I had to supply for myself." Unfolding his arms and sitting up, he looked at her earnestly, his voice becoming low. "It didn't know how pretty you are."

She flushed rapidly and was vastly relieved to see Faisal gliding forward bearing a large brass tray on one uplifted palm. He set their drinks down with practiced grace, looking at Spencer with unconcealed curiosity. "These are on the house," he said. "You two are perhaps celebrating some special occasion?"

"In a way." Spencer smiled broadly and turned to Emily. "I took the liberty of ordering the meal before you arrived. The best way to enjoy Moroccan food is to sample a little bit of everything."

She nodded in assent, and Faisal rubbed his hands together with relish. "Today I bring you all of our best dishes. I will be back in just a moment." He bustled off, leaving them alone again.

"Now, where were we?" Spencer said promptly. "Oh, yes, your vital statistics." Emily was speechless, and he mistook her silence for approval. "I think," he continued, "that all computers should carry that sort of information, don't you? However, this one neglected to describe your long silken hair, your unusually shaped eyes, that feline look that you try so futilely to subdue—"

Emily found her voice. "Look, Mr. McIntyre—"

"Spencer—please."

"If you don't mind," Emily went on firmly, "I think we should keep this conversation within professional limits. I'm afraid you don't understand my position."

"Afraid. You, afraid?" His tone became adamant.

"No, you're not. I don't believe you're afraid of anything. Not the lady who skied twelve miles cross-country in a blizzard."

Her mouth dropped open. "How did you know *that?*"

"You underestimate me—and my sources."

"No, I don't," she protested wryly, shaking her head in bewilderment. "You're a walking fountain of information." She eyed him suspiciously. "Just how friendly was that computer?"

"Very." He folded his arms in front of him, a look of distinct satisfaction on his lively face. "But you'll find out."

She stole a glance at him and saw that his shrewd gray eyes had lost their laserlike glare. Now they had the clear softness of a summer cloud, but they were twinkling with a roguish light. His fingers drummed the floor in time to the sensuous Middle Eastern music that swayed around them, and he clearly seemed to be enjoying himself. It didn't bother him at all that he was completely baffling her. She had no idea what to say to him, but was thankfully spared the effort when Faisal appeared, bearing a round brass platter.

He placed several covered dishes in front of them with an enthusiastic smile and produced a basket of flat, round pita bread. After handing them two hot towels, he wished them a hearty appetite and, as quickly as he had come, glided off, leaving them to survey the food. Spencer leaned forward, examining the meal with interest, and pointed at the various dishes.

"This is couscous, the national dish," he explained. "This is hummus—a chick pea paste, this is tabboule salad, and here we have stuffed grape leaves."

Emily looked at Spencer expectantly. "Uh—didn't he forget something?"

"What?"

"Plates. Knives. Forks." She gestured helplessly. "We can't eat with our hands."

Clear, spontaneous laughter bubbled up inside of him.

"What's so funny?" she asked plaintively.

"This is a completely authentic Moroccan restaurant. We shall eat as the Moroccans eat."

She watched in astonishment as he dipped a piece of the flat pita bread into the hummus and swirled it around, popping it into his mouth. "Try the salad," he nodded encouragingly. "And don't worry about getting messy. This is a delightfully sensual way to eat, and there are hot towels to wipe your hands with."

She laughed self-consciously and picked out a sprig of mint and a piece of tomato from the tabboule plate, nibbling the combination from her fingers. "Delicious," she pronounced. "What's this?" she added, pointing at the couscous.

"A stew made from chicken, lamb, pasta and vegetables," he answered obligingly.

She took a piece of chicken and ate it slowly, relishing the unusual blend of flavors. Next she tried the hummus, swirling a chunk of pita bread through the thick paste and sucking the warm, spicy mixture from her hand.

As the meal continued, she lost her sense of shyness, and she leaned back and drank in the heady atmosphere enthusiastically. The absence of eating utensils gave her a new sense of freedom that was gently aided by the dry white wine.

Spencer looked at her across the small table several minutes later as he tore the meat from a chicken leg with his teeth. "Now I see why you'd like this place," he said with a confiding air.

"Don't tell me the computer said I'd like it," she said incredulously. "That I won't believe."

"Believe what you wish. I asked for a restaurant that would provide a highly relaxing atmosphere and bring out the best of your character. I think I'm starting to understand why this place was chosen for you."

She sipped her wine, and her eyes lit up with impish curiosity. "And are you seeing the best of my character?" she challenged.

"Almost," he answered after a short pause during which the steel crept back into his gaze. "But I'm still waiting for the spontaneity."

"I am very spontaneous," she announced stiffly, and he laughed.

"Don't be ridiculous. You haven't done one spontaneous thing since you got here."

"Neither have you," she countered. "In fact, you've been quite calculating."

He frowned, considering. An idea lit his changeable features, and he leaned over her, his face only inches from hers. She drew back instinctively, but the power in his clear blue eyes was riveting. She knew what was going to happen, and as much as she knew she shouldn't allow it, she simply couldn't resist. He supported his weight with his arms, the corded muscles tightening against the fabric of his shirt, and his eyes slowly raked her face, making very sure that he was causing the desired effect.

Emily's lips parted unconsciously, giving Spencer all the invitation he needed. The space between them closed as he gently kissed her. Without volition her eyes closed completely. Her hands went blindly to his arms in an attempt to hold him at bay, but the feel of the muscular power beneath stopped her. He responded quickly, cradling her head in one hand and letting his mouth explore hers with languid sensuality.

He tasted of warm honey, and her heartbeat quickened. But the moment his mouth shifted from hers,

Emily ducked her head, still keenly aware that she was skating on very thin ice.

Spencer regarded her for a moment, his eyes assessing her from beneath veiled lids. "Was that spontaneous enough for you?" he asked huskily. She couldn't answer. "Or is this?" He kissed her again, giving her no chance to escape. This time his arms encircled her, lightly tracing the curve of her hips before settling on the small of her back. She caught the warm, woody scent of him as he pressed her back. Her head touched one of the pillows as the Middle Eastern music intensified and washed over them. Reason returned.

She couldn't possibly allow herself to be swept shamelessly away in this calculated setting. Not with Spencer McIntyre. Not like this. It was too fast, too incongruous—too dangerous. McIntyre was known for never playing by the rules, and Emily had been taught to believe in rules. She pushed him gently but firmly away, and she sat up awkwardly, quickly smoothing her hair into place.

"What is it, Emily?" Spencer whispered, trying to kiss the side of her neck. "Don't worry."

"This is completely uncalled for!" she said, forcing herself to calm down. Slowly her senses stopped spinning. "This was supposed to be a job interview."

"Oh, is that what you're worried about?" He smiled. "Well, don't. You're already hired."

His casual confidence only increased her trepidation. "But—but I never said I would take the job. I'm not even sure I want it. Especially now," she added pointedly. His hands were still draped around the back of her neck, and she reached up and pried them away.

He sat back, disappointed. "And we were getting along so well."

"Look, Mr. McIntyre—"

"Spencer."

"All right. Spencer. I think that perhaps it would be best if I just went home and forgot this whole thing."

Suddenly, he was all business again, the laser gleam returning to his eyes. "You can't do that," he stated with finality.

"Why not?" she asked in astonishment.

"Because I want you. And I don't take no for an answer."

His self-assurance was maddening. "Well, you can't have me," she retorted icily.

"Listen, Emily," he said calmly, leaning forward. "You are the best person for this job. Of that I have no doubt. And besides, the pay is fantastic. Why should you say no?"

She found herself floundering. "I don't even know what the job *is*," she protested.

He shrugged. "The usual. A client with a problem. But that's not important."

"It is to me," she insisted.

He sighed. "All right." His gaze was laced with something very like admiration, and she realized that he never *did* take no for an answer.

"I'll tell you what," he continued, sitting back and regarding her coolly. "My client is giving a party tonight, and I'm supposed to be there. Why don't you come with me, and you can make up your mind later on."

She hesitated. "Is this a date or what? I think you should know right now that I never mix business with pleasure."

"Okay, okay. It's not a date. We'll call it a business engagement."

His impatience amused her for some reason. He was so obviously used to getting his own way. "Good," she answered demurely.

"But the business part of the evening ends promptly at midnight," he added ominously.

"Oh?" She arched an eyebrow. "And what happens then? I turn into a pumpkin?"

"Maybe." He didn't bat an eye. "If you like."

Faisal came through the curtain carrying a tall, elaborate teapot and two small cups. They fell silent as he lifted the brass pot and ceremoniously poured the hot, sweet Moroccan tea, letting it fall in a long stream into the cups.

Emily tasted it and found it unexpectedly thick. It coursed through her body like warm honey, causing a sigh of contentment to escape her. Spencer watched her, his eyes flashing over the rim of his cup.

"I'll pick you up at eight tonight," he said.

"All right," she relented. There was no point in arguing with him. "I live at—"

"I know your address," he said shortly.

"Oh. Of course."

"And wear your hair down."

"*What?*"

He reached over and took the clasp from her hair, combing it gently through his fingers so that it fell around her shoulders like soft, sleek ribbons. "Much better," he pronounced. "Tonight, the real Emily is going to emerge."

In the taxi on the way back to Brooklyn Heights, Emily pondered the strange lunch and the dynamic man who was so full of riddles. She had no doubt that he was every bit as brilliant as he was rumored to be. But she also had no illusions about her own abilities. She was sure that in front of a computer terminal, she would be a match for him.

The taxi deposited her at the corner, and she walked

slowly down the busy street. She felt unaccountably restless, and she itched for some way to rid herself of the jumpy feeling. She passed the florist, stopping to admire the bright spots of color in the window, and walked by the bookstore and the hardware store with a slight frown on her face. Large color photographs of fabulously coiffured models in the window of the hairdresser's caught her eye, and she paused. Spencer's remark about her hair still needled her. Who was he to tell her how to wear her hair? Some demon inside of her pushed her to open the door and walk inside.

A dazzling receptionist with long, painted fingernails looked up and smiled. "May I help you?" she asked in a Bronx accent.

Emily hesitated. "I don't have an appointment . . . but if you're not too busy, I—I'd like to get a haircut."

The receptionist flipped through her appointment book and nodded. "Well, I think we can take you. What kind of cut do you want?" She eyed Emily's long, silky tresses. "A trim?"

"No," Emily answered recklessly. "I want a pixie cut. A short pixie cut." Her glance fell to the woman's hands. "And a manicure," she added, throwing her last shred of caution out the window. "The works."

Chapter Three

"What did you do to your hair?"

Emily's hand flew involuntarily to her head, and she brushed a few of the new short wisps into place. The unaccustomed lightness was still startling, but she knew that the short pixie cut framed her face in a new and beguiling way. But his appearance was equally surprising. He was dressed in an exquisitely tailored suit that was tapered close to his lean body, and he was lounging casually against the door frame with a crooked grin on his face.

"I had it cut," she answered faintly, staring back at him.

"I can see that," he said patiently. "But why?"

Her only response was a sly, feline smile that clearly pointed to him as the culprit.

He got the message loud and clear and shot her an admiring glance. "You're full of surprises, Emily. Just as I thought."

"And you're not?" She looked him over from head to toe, standing back as if admiring a rare painting. "I'm surprised you even own a suit. And by the looks of it, I'd say it's hardly ever been worn."

"You're right," he said cheerfully. "I just bought it this afternoon."

"Well, there's a first time for everything," she returned breezily.

He chuckled lightly as they went out of the building. A cab was waiting for them by the curb.

"I don't know why," Emily said as she looked at the cab, "but somehow I expected a BMW or some flashy foreign car."

"Not my style," he said as he opened the door for her. "I like things practical. Besides, I don't like to own things. It's too much trouble."

"Well, this is certainly practical," she said dubiously, eyeing the battered yellow taxi. She looked at the driver, who was taking in their conversation with relish.

"Where to now, Spence?" he asked, surprising Emily with the familiarity.

"Sutton Place, the Sheridan Manor."

The driver shifted into gear and they lurched off.

"'Spence'?" she repeated. "You two know each other?"

"Al," Spencer said, "this is the girl I was telling you about. Emily, this is Al Sherman."

"How ya doin', Emily?" Al glanced up at the rear-view mirror and caught Emily's gaze. She smiled back politely at his reflection.

"Al and I go back a long way together," Spencer said. "He's the only cab driver in town who gives credit."

"Credit?" she repeated, trying to keep up with their banter.

"When I first went out on my own," Spencer explained, "I didn't have any money. Just credit cards."

"No cash?" she asked.

"No cash. I started my consulting firm with a very tight budget. Al was nice enough to trust me for the money, and for the first three months of my fledging company, he drove me all over town." He flashed Al an appreciative smile.

"Sounds pretty risky to me."

"Not really. In those days, I used my hotel room as an office. I had one good suit, some decent stationery and my trusty friend and business adviser driving me all over New York." He gestured grandly to Al in the front seat.

"It looks as though nothing has changed," Emily observed wryly.

"On the contrary," he said, laughing. "Now I have hotel suites in every major city, a band of trusty cab drivers who speak ten different languages, better stationery and—" He smiled. "Even some cash."

"And one good suit," she added mischievously, turning to admire the view of the skyline as they drove over the bridge.

"Actually," he said, "I bought this suit for a very special occasion."

She turned back and looked at him. "Really? This client is that important?"

"I mean," he explained, "this date is very important."

"Date?" She sat up in alarm. "What date?"

"We won't be staying long at the party. We'll just put in an appearance. I don't have too much patience with old-money types and aristocrats. I thought we'd go somewhere for a late dinner and maybe catch the sunrise. I know this great little stretch of deserted beach, and—"

"Sorry," she cut in, her tone deliberately dampening. "But this is supposed to be strictly business, remember?"

"It is," he assured her, "but only for a while. I thought we could—"

"Mix business with pleasure?" She smiled and firmly shook her head. "Forget it. You are embarking on hiring your first employee, so make your choice. Business or pleasure?" She knew she was taking a decided risk by pressing that question, but she wanted a definite answer. It was becoming increasingly difficult to deny her attraction to this mercurial man. Perhaps it would be best if they forgot about the business part of it altogether and turned the evening into a conventional social one.

But he surprised her by sitting back and deeply contemplating her question.

"She's right, Spence," Al agreed heartily. "You better forget all about that party. I can take the Triborough Bridge to Grand Central Parkway and have you on that beach in less than an hour, if that's what you want. Besides, I'm in the mood for a night swim. It's been a hot day."

Spencer started to laugh, but Emily was not amused. "This is not funny," she said, trying to sound stern. Suddenly, she was seized with a new insecurity. These two men were like old army buddies, and she felt oddly out of place. Perhaps Spencer wasn't really that interested in her. Maybe he really did need her professional help, and she should stick to that and ignore his innuendoes. She leaned forward and tapped Al on the shoulder. "You stay on course for Sutton Place," she ordered. "And you—" She pointed at Spencer.

"Yes?" he asked, still chuckling.

"You better watch yourself tonight. This is serious business."

Again, he surprised her by dropping his boyish mirth and frowning solemnly. "You're right. It's worth about a quarter of a million dollars, as a matter of fact."

She swallowed hard, letting this information sink in. "Really?" she asked, trying not to sound as impressed as she was. "Then don't you think you should tell me something about the client?"

"What would you like to know?" he asked coolly,

and Emily looked at him in frustration. How could he be so cool and calm about a quarter of a million dollars?

"Well, for openers," she sputtered, "what is the nature of the problem? What kind of company is it? What does the man in charge expect of us? Should we talk about something neutral to break the ice, or should we just come right out and talk about the computer problem?"

Spencer met her barrage of questions with a bemused smile. "First of all," he said slowly, "don't bring up the problem that he's having. It's rather—uh, embarrassing to him, and he doesn't like to talk about it. He hasn't actually lost any money so far, but the computer has become very—how can I describe it?" He gave up and laughed shortly, shaking his head.

"Is it that funny?" Emily asked, searching his face.

"Let's just say that the computer has developed a . . . complication. It has become harder to work with. She's turned into an emotional bunch of quivering circuits."

"She?" Emily arched an eyebrow. "Again, it's a she."

Both Spencer and Al burst into loud laughter. "Yes," Spencer answered decidedly, "it's definitely a she."

Emily still had the uncomfortable feeling that she was being left out of some private joke, one that she wasn't sure she wanted to know about. So she sat back against the seat, looking out the window in a detached sort of way, letting Spencer enjoy himself in his own odd way.

As the cab sped along the East Side Highway, she could see the United Nations Building up ahead and, just beyond it, the exclusive area known as Sutton Place. She'd never been there, and she looked forward to seeing it for the first time with a little tingle of anticipation.

Sutton Place faced the East River, and it was lined with luxurious townhouses and apartment buildings. As they turned on to the short but beautiful street, the cab slowed to a crawl. Each imposing façade reflected the taste and refinement of its owner. The evidence of enormous wealth was everywhere as they pulled up in front of the last house on the block, if it could be called a block. The street was crowded with parked limousines, the drivers chatting casually with one another as they waited for their employers.

As Emily and Spencer got out of the cab, she looked up to the left, where the Queensborough Bridge towered gracefully across the river.

"Nice little neighborhood," Spencer remarked as he escorted her to the entrance. "All it lacks is a corner grocery store."

Emily smiled as they climbed the few steps in front. She was a little nervous, and something told her that he was, too. But while her anxiety stemmed from the material environment, his seemed to be detached, as if where they were didn't affect him at all. Her suspicion was well founded, for as they reached the top of the steps, he suddenly turned to her. It was the first time he had been totally serious on this outing, his expression pointedly concerned.

"We won't stay long," he said, clearly giving an order. "I want to get this over with as soon as possible. I'm not crazy about these affairs, and this one will be typical."

"Why?" she asked, surprised.

He gestured to the limousines that were double-parked in the street. "A few of my clients are here tonight."

"So?" she persisted. "Why should that make you nervous?"

He looked startled for a moment, and then he smiled, the tension vanishing. She looked even more puzzled at the swift change in him, and he threw her a sympathetic grin. "Don't worry," he assured her. "There's something I haven't told you yet, that's all. I was hoping to broach the subject before we got this far, but somehow it seemed best to do it this way."

She still had no idea what he was talking about. "Are you getting cold feet?" she asked. If he was, she wanted to know now.

He answered the question with a request. "Just promise me one thing."

"What?" she asked darkly. "I'm not sure I like this."

"That doesn't matter," he said, waving her insecurity aside. "What matters is that you're working for me now, and this is all a matter of business.

His answer didn't suit her at all. Obviously something was up, and she intended to find out what it was before she walked into the party and made a fool of herself. "Spencer," she said firmly, "either you tell me what's going on, or I'm leaving." To underline her words, she turned and started down the steps.

His hand reached out and clasped hers so that she couldn't leave. Reluctantly, she climbed back up and stood next to him, her eyes still demanding an answer. She squirmed her fingers free of his and looked up at him expectantly.

"If you want an answer," he said calmly, "you'll have to find it in there." He pointed at the door. "All I'll tell you is that our host has a serious problem with his computer—"

"And you can't handle it alone," she finished impatiently. "I know that already."

"Well?" he said, gesturing elaborately to the door. "Are we going to stand here arguing all evening, or shall we go in?"

She thought for a moment, waiting deliberately to annoy him. "Yes," she answered finally, "but I'm not going as your employee. As of this moment, I'm strictly independent."

"That doesn't matter," he said airily. "You're here because of me."

A tinge of anger flashed through her. The last thing she needed was to be ordered around by him. Making a fast decision, she stepped forward and jammed her finger onto the doorbell.

"That's what I like about you, Emily," he teased. "You're quick on your feet."

She ignored him and smiled graciously as the door was opened by a uniformed maid. The gentle sound of chamber music emanated from inside, mingling with the low hum of cultured voices.

"Hello," Spencer said. "I'm Spencer McIntyre." He turned to Emily. "And this is Emily Moreau . . ." He hesitated for a second, and Emily shot him a meaningful glance. "My associate," he finished. She nodded, pleased with his choice of words.

"Please come in," the maid said. They followed her into a small foyer that opened into an enormous living room that was three quarters the length of the house. Well-dressed people were milling about, and Emily knew at one glance that they were not ordinary millionaires. She was looking at very old money. Everything was understated, with no showiness or flash, and it was this very sense of restraint that made the impression so imposing. These people did not need to display their opulence; they were too accustomed to it to want to put it on display. But of course it was there nonetheless, evident in the dry, modulated voices, the simple but elegant clothing, and the occasional flash of a very old, priceless gem.

"What a lovely home," Emily said sincerely, her eyes darting everywhere. The maid smiled wryly, as if used to buffering the first-time reactions of new guests, but all she said was "I'll take your coat." Emily was still looking around avidly, stopping once to stare wide-eyed at an original Renoir that was hanging on the wall. She unbuttoned her lightweight coat and let the maid slip it from her shoulders, completely unaware of the effect it had on her escort. So mesmerized was she by her surroundings that she had forgotten how she had chosen to complete the new image started by the impromptu haircut. Under the plain cotton coat was a simple but dynamic black dress, the low neck emphasized by a length of taffeta ruffle. As Emily's slender arms were bared and her hands emerged, the sparkling red nails flashed right in front of Spencer's face.

"Holy mackerel!" he said, not bothering to hide his reaction. Emily looked startled for a moment, and then she smiled coolly. His frank gaze swept over her, obviously liking what he saw, and the maid suppressed a grin as she glided off.

"Is something the matter?" Emily asked with a straight face.

"Uh—no, no," he answered hastily. "You look—uh —very nice," he finished, his eyes still glued to the subtle but distinct curves under the dress.

They turned to face the party, and all at once Emily found her courage flagging. She still had no idea whose house it was or why they were there, and suddenly she found Spencer a very welcome addition. She took his arm without a word, clinging to it firmly so that he wouldn't dart off and leave her standing there, and her insecurity was not abated when she spied a small sculpture of a ballerina that she realized with a jolt was an original Degas.

"Our host seems to like French impressionism," she murmured, trying not to sound as awed as she was.

He didn't answer, but he squeezed her arm gently, his fingers lingering for a moment as they walked into the living room. Spencer led her over to the bar, where he gallantly got her a glass of white wine. She accepted it gratefully, sipping slowly as they stood looking around.

They didn't have to wait long before someone recognized Spencer. A wizened old man in the corner saw him and made a beeline for them, his face opening in greeting.

"Well, well, Mr. McIntyre," he said. "I should have known you would be here. Whenever a computer breaks down, you're not far behind." He glanced at Emily, his eyes crinkling in appreciation at her youth and striking appearance. Leaning toward her conspiratorially, he whispered, "The Lone Ranger, that's what he is." She realized that he was talking about Spencer, and she smiled politely. "He helped me out of a very sticky situation some years back," the man continued. "Seems I had lost my payroll somewhere inside of one of those dad-blamed machines. That computer simply refused to pay all of my employees!" He chuckled merrily, as if the whole thing were a pleasant joke. But Emily sympathized with all of those people not receiving their paychecks. This garrulous old man was probably another J. P. Fenton underneath his easygoing exterior. She stole a glance at Spencer and was gratified to see that he wasn't smiling, either.

"How are you, Mr. Winchester?" Spencer asked finally.

"Fine, young man, just fine," he answered jovially. "I took your advice, you know, and put a whole new batch of computers into my Tokyo office. But I was hoping you'd be the one to set up the new system for me." He frowned suddenly, some of the affability falling away. Then he turned to Emily, as if to gain her as an ally. "This is a hard man to find. Here one minute, gone the next."

Emily was surprised that Spencer had not made any introductions. He remained aloof, but the old man didn't give up so easily, and she realized that he was trying to pry some sort of information out of Spencer. Her suspicion was immediately confirmed.

"I'll come right to the point, McIntyre," he said with sudden sharpness. "I expected you to program those computers for me. You know Japanese well enough, so I understand, and you were in Tokyo four times in the past year without once stopping by. I should think you'd have time for—"

Spencer stopped him with a cold stare. "I'm a very busy man, Mr. Winchester. We had a contract, and I fulfilled it. I'm a problem solver, not a programmer. You hired me to get your payroll into working order, and I did." He took a swallow of wine and nodded curtly, leading Emily away. "If you'll excuse us," he said with frigid politeness.

Emily was shocked by his behavior, but she decided not to jump to conclusions. She was the stranger there, after all. "Wasn't that a little . . . abrupt?" she ventured.

He jerked his head back to glance at Winchester. "Don't let him fool you. He may look like a sweet old man, but he's actually a very spoiled old man, and a bad manager to boot. He inherited a perfectly good company and has been driving it into the ground for years. That was the only way to get rid of him, believe me."

"But—but couldn't you be just a little more tactful?" she asked, still holding onto his arm.

He looked at her quizzically. "That will be your department, Emily," he decided. "I'll leave that all up to you."

"Oh. Thanks very much."

His face softened. "What Winchester just doesn't understand is that I am not a programmer. I'm a glorified mechanic, a computer doctor who makes house calls. When I fix whatever is wrong, I take to my heels."

"Speaking of heels," Emily said, "didn't Fenton want you to do some programming for him?"

He gripped her arm suddenly and looked around quickly. "Never mind that now," he said tersely. "I don't do programming, and that's all. It's bad for my image."

"What image is that? The Lone Ranger?"

His grip tightened. "Come on, Tonto. Let's go mingle with the jet set."

He led her through the party to the back of the room, where two French doors opened onto a huge and brilliantly lit patio, thronged with people. A waiter passed with a tray of canapés, and Emily nibbled on one and took another glass of wine. They didn't have to wait long for another conversation to ensue; everyone seemed to know Spencer or know of him, and Emily soon found herself involved in a spirited discussion about yachts with two stout women bedecked in diamonds.

"So there we were," one woman was saying in lofty tones, "on this adorable little island off the Greek coast. And can you imagine it? The yacht simply refused to start! My husband had an important business meeting in Athens the next day, and there we were, marooned on a yacht in the middle of the Mediterranean!"

Emily smiled politely, and the other woman clucked sympathetically. "Well, we simply had to get out of there, and you'll never guess what we did." Her eyes sparkled, challenging them to guess.

"You radioed for a helicopter," Spencer volunteered. She shook her head, a little girl with a secret. "You . . . uh—you hailed a passing ocean liner," he continued patiently.

Emily beamed suddenly. "There's only one way to do it, then," she announced, deflating the suspense. "Just hop aboard one of the native fishing boats. The locals do it all the time. If you don't mind the smell, they'll take you anywhere you want to go, for a fee."

They all looked at Emily in surprise, and the woman telling the story hid a flicker of annoyance. "Well, that's exactly what we did," she said, trying to regain her momentum. "It was just dreadful. By the time we reached the mainland, we smelled like I don't *know* what. I never forgave Godfrey for that."

Emily chuckled. "It is quite an experience," she agreed. "My father and I spent a lot of time on the southern coast of Greece. It's very earthy, of course, and the people are absolutely wonderful. One night our jeep broke down, and we slept in a barn with the cows. The next day, they drove us all the way back to the base, on the other side of the island."

The women nodded politely, but Spencer's eyebrow shot up. "Jeep?" he asked. "Base? What base?"

"Army jeeps," she explained. "Ditto for the base."

"I didn't know that," he said accusingly, as if she should have told him about it before.

"Computers don't know everything, after all." Emily grinned, and the two women smiled, grasping at the new straw in the conversation.

"But Spencer knows everything about computers," said the other woman smoothly. He saved my husband's company from utter ruin, didn't you?" She smiled sweetly at Spencer, who accepted the compliment modestly.

"Oh, I don't know, Mrs. Stanton," he said. "All I did was get the bugs out. It was really a routine job."

The first woman gazed at him doubtfully. "I hear that this one isn't quite so simple," she said ominously. "Our host tells me that it's of a rather . . . unusual nature." Her voice was almost taunting. She was trying to get him to tell her the juicy details, but Spencer wasn't biting. He continued to gaze back at her placidly, forcing her to go on. "My husband said that even you may not be able to fix this one, Mr. McIntyre."

His smile remained perfectly neutral. "Your husband has been wrong about me before, Mrs. Winchester," he said evenly.

"Well," she huffed, "I wish you the best of luck, I'm sure." The two women sauntered off.

"What is going on here?" Emily hissed the moment they were gone. "Everyone seems to know about this latest computer problem except me. I don't even know whose house this is!"

He leaned back against the door frame, regarding her with an amused expression. Then he laughed to himself. "You certainly told Mrs. Winchester!"

"I didn't realize that was Winchester's wife," she said. "You should have told me."

"Why? And miss out on all this entertainment?" He laughed again. "You were right about tact, Emily. It's definitely your department."

He took her arm, and they began to circulate again,

hobnobbing with the glittering array of guests. An hour passed pleasantly enough, during which Spencer continued to chat amiably in his breezy manner, and Emily continued to alternately startle and impress him with her unexpected revelations and her uncanny ability to gentle his occasionally abrupt remarks. What was interesting was that so many of these people seemed to know Spencer, and yet he was not one of them, not really.

He'd helped most of them out with knotty computer problems, for which all of them were unabashedly grateful. But he remained aloof, an independent spirit who was there because he chose to be there, not because he was obliged to. The other guests treated him with respect, but the respect was mingled with an awe that bordered on uncertainty. It was as if no one was quite sure who he was exactly, but it didn't matter, because his talents were so valuable and they could afford to pay for them.

After her third glass of wine, Emily felt pleasantly lightheaded, and she chatted easily with the guests. She had all but forgotten about Spencer's important client despite the occasional leading remarks about the delicate nature of his particular problem. When Spencer was ready to reveal the nature of their visit, he would. In the meantime, it would look too ridiculous to ask someone whose party it was, so she sipped her wine and waited for the mystery to solve itself.

And she had to admit that it was certainly enjoyable being with Spencer McIntyre. He had an air of authority in the group that was appealing because it was so carefree. Spencer didn't owe anybody anything, and he didn't expect any favors. He looked absolutely devastating in that suit, circulating casually among the multimillionaires and their pampered wives, talking about complicated business matters one minute and indulgently listening to descriptions of social soirées the next. His hand remained almost constantly at her elbow, and she liked the warm, dependable feel of it. She even got used to wearing the revealing black dress, discovering curves in her figure that she hadn't known were there.

After an hour of congenial mingling, Emily found herself back in the house listening to a conversation about Swiss bank accounts. Spencer was making a forceful point, gesturing repeatedly with his free hand, when suddenly he caught sight of something that made him dry up in midsentence.

"What is it?" Emily asked.

"Our gracious host." His hand tightened around his drink.

Emily peered through the crowd but couldn't see anyone who looked intimidating. Her glance fell on Mrs. Winchester, who gave her a cool nod.

They moved away from their group, Emily still looking around curiously. "Who is it?" she demanded. "It's about time I was introduced, don't you think?"

Then she noticed the short, aggressive figure of a man approaching them. She turned to Spencer, instantly curious. Who was this man that he could make Spencer tense up so suddenly? She had seen Spencer handle the likes of Winchester and his cronies with ease. Why should this one man be different?

But when the man came nearer and she stared with unmasked curiosity at his face, she was the one who froze. It was J. P. Fenton.

"Oh, my God," she groaned through her teeth. "Why didn't you tell me? I could kill you for this!"

"Kill me later," he whispered back, his hand gripping her arm as if to prevent her from bolting. "Just play along for now, all right? Don't tell him you ever worked for him before. I'll break it to him gently later on."

Before she had a chance to retort with some suitably cutting remark, Fenton was upon them, his sharp, beady eyes moving from Spencer's face to hers. He had an air of authority that was all too familiar to her. He moved like a commanding officer about to send a platoon on a secret mission.

"I hope you haven't been spilling the beans" was the first thing he said to Spencer. "Come out to the patio. I don't want anyone eavesdropping." He turned and marched outside, letting them follow behind as they wended their way through the crowd.

Soft stars glittered in the dark sky, and a small tugboat was making its way down the East River. It was a peaceful, idyllic scene, but they were not going to be allowed to enjoy it. Fenton led them to the edges of the party.

Emily cut him a quick, curious glance, wondering what the problem was that they had been called in to fix. Spencer had already updated and streamlined the system. That much she knew, of course, because she had been one of the unwilling victims. She hadn't even known that he was still working for Fenton. She assumed that his contract there had already ended. But apparently there was more to the computers there than she had been privileged to know about.

Fenton caught her looking at him, and she looked away at once. He didn't remember her, mostly because he had never really met her. She had seen him stalking around the company like the imperious general that he was, leaving ranks of nervous employees "looking busy" in his wake, but they had never been introduced, and he had never bothered to get to know any of his lower-echelon employees.

"This is Emily Moreau," Spencer was saying smoothly. "My new associate."

Fenton's shrewd eyes were upon her, but there was no spark of recognition. "Associate, eh?" He looked her up and down. "Do you have an address?" he asked abruptly.

"I beg your pardon?" she returned faintly.

"An address," he repeated sternly. "You know, a house with a mailbox."

"Uh—why, yes. I live in an apartment in Brooklyn Heights."

"Good," he said gruffly. "Do you know why you're here?"

She looked at Spencer and shook her head helplessly. "To tell you the truth, no. I just got back from a vacation, and Spencer here called me and told me you had a problem."

"A problem?" He arched a glance at Spencer, who was leaning calmly against the side of the house. "Yes, I certainly have a problem. It's such a grievous one that even the great Mr. McIntyre here can't solve it for me."

He seemed to be challenging her, and she decided to meet him on his own ground. "I see," she said. "Then why not fire him if he can't help you?"

Spencer's head shot up at this, and Fenton seemed mildly amused. But his reaction was quickly buried under a dissatisfied frown.

"He can't fire me," Spencer answered for him. "It would be too scandalous. If the rest of the business world heard that Fenton's computer had a problem so tricky that even I couldn't solve it, the stock market alone would eliminate him. Not to mention the fact that he'd be a laughingstock of New York." He smiled grimly. "So he's stuck with me. And now he's got you to contend with." He stood up, suddenly in command. "Look here, Fenton. Emily is the best person I know for this problem. She's familiar with your system, and I know she can get your computer back to normal. Or at least operational."

"It's not even operational?" she asked. This was worse than she had thought.

"It's operational, all right," Fenton answered. *"Too* operational. And from this moment on, you'll refer to this problem as a minor flaw in the program—nothing more. I can't afford bad publicity, and if I hear any, I'll have you two to blame." He stopped and looked at them, making sure they had understood his meaning. "The system works fine, Ms. Moreau. All of the proper information is intact, and it is accessible without any hitch." He spoke firmly, emphasizing his words.

"I see," she said carefully. "Then is it the speed that is presenting you with a—uh—flaw?" She didn't like this cat and mouse conversation. She wished he would just tell her what he wanted her to do without all the double talk. Then she would know whether or not she could do it at all. The computer had been functioning fine the day she had left. She couldn't imagine what was wrong with it now. It gave her a curious sensation to know that this very powerful man was completely at the mercy of her talents, and she waited curiously to hear what he would tell her.

"Uh, no, not exactly," Fenton replied evasively. "Well, actually, it does have something to do with the speed, but not exactly . . ." He paused, searching for the right words. "I would say that the speed is greatly reduced at the moment, yes."

But the answer was still much too vague. She needed more concrete information. "Just what is it you want me to do?" she asked bluntly.

"I think it would be best," Spencer broke in gently, "if Emily simply came with me to the company tomorrow morning and took a look for herself. Then we'll let her make up her mind if she wants to tackle the job or not."

Fenton thought about that and realized he had no choice. "All right," he said sternly. "But I want you to stay here for a while and mingle." Emily looked at him quizzically. "Two of my competitors are here, and so are three of my top clients. I don't want them to think that anything is wrong, and it's up to the two of you to confirm that impression. I've been able to keep this out of the papers up till now, and I intend to keep it that way. Is that clear?" He looked at each of them, one at a time, and they both nodded gravely. Emily could see why he was the president of a multinational company. When he gave orders, people listened. "I want your answer by noon tomorrow, Ms. Moreau," he concluded. And then he walked off, leaving them to mull over what had just transpired.

"Well, now you've met old man Fenton himself," Spencer said. "What do you think?"

She wheeled on him. "You should have told me! You should have told me that Fenton was still your client!"

"I couldn't do that." He shrugged. "I promised Fenton I would keep this all a hush-hush operation."

She frowned. "But why me? Why do I deserve this great honor?" she asked, a touch sarcastically.

"It is a great honor, as a matter of fact," he said seriously. "I simply asked the computer to give me the name of the person best qualified to handle this job. Your name was number one on the list."

"But—but it seems so odd to be going back there as a consultant when I was an employee only two weeks ago!"

Spencer laughed. "Oh, knock it off, Emily. Stop being so rank and file. You're an independent now, and Fenton needs you. He probably always needed you, but you never let him know it. You know that system as well as anyone, probably better. So what's your problem?"

"I see. Fenton uses his computer to fire me, and now you use it again to rehire me. Very convenient."

"Maybe I had other reasons," he said, his eyes twinkling devilishly. She looked away instinctively in a futile effort to avoid his provocative look, but he wasn't deterred. "Why don't we get out of here and go for a late dinner. I know this great little place—"

"Forget it," she said, crushing the end of the invitation. "No mixing business with pleasure, remember?" She faced him squarely, with far more confidence than she was feeling.

"Ah, yes. Then I take it you'll accept the job?"

She hesitated, aware of the trap he had set and admiring his skill in leading her into it. The glint in his gray eyes reflected his keen intelligence as he watched her every move.

"You think you're pretty smart, don't you?" she asked finally, already knowing who had won.

"Yes," he answered without arrogance. "So what'll it be, Emily?" He smiled again, very gently this time, stroking her cheek with one finger. "Either way I win. So say yes."

His touch was amazingly powerful. She could scarcely believe that such a delicate, innocent stroke could be so disturbing, and yet she felt her blood begin to tingle and spin in a breathless reaction. "Yes," she said hastily, turning her face away. His smile of triumph almost blinded her.

Emily tried to analyze the evening as the cab sped up the East Side Highway, but it was impossible. She still didn't know what kind of problem Fenton could be having with his computer, but oddly enough, that didn't seem to be the issue. In a way, she was glad he was having difficulties after firing so many good people, but now that she had met him personally, she almost felt sorry for him. So much seemed to rest on his public image, on what people said and thought about him.

"Don't you think Fenton will be upset that we left so early?" she asked.

Spencer knitted his hands behind his head and leaned back. "He's not fooling anyone, and he knows it. Those people at the party tonight are a lot smarter than they appear, Winchester included. They didn't come for a chatty social evening, believe me. They came to find out how their investments with Fenton International Industries are doing. All of them know that if they withdraw their money and sell their stock, the company would be in serious trouble."

"They're all stockholders?"

He nodded. "Of course. And very large shareholders, at that. Fenton is the chairman of the board, but he's not just a figurehead." He sat up and turned to her. "He inherited the company from his grandfather, but he's no Winchester. He knows that business backwards and forwards. I wouldn't be surprised if half the information stored in the computer is already lodged permanently in his head."

"You sound as if you really like him," she remarked.

"Liking has nothing to do with it. He's the last of a dying breed—the twentieth-century tycoon. He's one of the men who built up a big industry and kept it big, without any help from a bunch of Harvard graduates with their MBAs and statistical reports."

"But—but you went to Harvard!" she protested, not understanding him at all.

"True," he said smugly. "But I only use it when I have to." She stared at him in bewilderment, and he smiled. "You're witnessing a changing of the guard,

Emily. In the old days, a man was shown a bunch of reports, and he made a decision. Today, the same reports are fed into a computer, and the human factor is never even considered."

"And J. P. Fenton has fallen under his own computer's spell," Emily said.

"More likely he was manipulated by it. I've seen it happen too many times not to recognize it. Even old pros like Fenton stand in awe of modern technology. They don't trust their own street smarts, even after all these years. They think a big and fancy machine knows more than they do about their own businesses. Maybe they think it's good management, but the trouble is, they divorce themselves from people so much that they no longer know what's going on."

Emily frowned. "You have it all figured out, don't you?"

"I've had a lot of time to think about it, that's all. I'm a doctor who makes house calls, remember? The problem isn't always in the computer. Sometimes it's in someone's head." He shrugged. "But there's nothing wrong with that. No one can know how to do everything, as long as they are smart enough to hire the person who is best at what they themselves can't do. If you surround yourself with the best, you're a good manager."

Emily looked at him shrewdly. "And are you a good manager?" she asked.

"I don't have to be," he answered a shade too quickly, and she knew that she had found a source of conflict in him. "I'm a loner by choice," he added. "It's easier that way. Less complicated. My billing system is child's play—a flat fee for each job, decided in advance."

"Nothing is that simple," she said slowly, watching

him. "What about all those jobs you turn down? I'm sure Winchester's company isn't the only one. You could have hired programmers to set up a system for him in Japan, but you didn't. How many other jobs have you turned down?"

"What difference does it make?" he demanded, turning to look out the window. "I'm making enough money. I'm doing exactly what I want. What's wrong with that?" He sounded defensive, almost peevish in his insistence.

"I just don't understand why you turn away business, that's all," she answered in a small voice. She didn't understand everything he was saying. It was just that something didn't ring true, and she was determined to find out what it was.

He was silent for a long moment. "I don't want to complicate my life," he said finally. "I'm not in this business for power or empire building. I like my freedom." He spoke with such intense conviction that she couldn't help but believe him. "Do you know what it's like to just stop your whole routine and take a chance?" He turned to face her, his eyes shining. "I'll bet you don't. Let me tell you about it. It's worth all the money and power in the world. And it's so simple. All you have to do is say no." He smiled an odd little smile. "That's the whole secret, but most people never even try it. Can you say no, Emily?"

She floundered. "Well, sure. Of course. What do you mean?"

He sat back, thinking for a moment. Then his eyes lit up with an example. "How many times did you go to work on a beautiful, cloudless day, the sun shining, the beach only an hour away, but you were stuck inside that morgue at Fenton International Industries?"

Emily said nothing. The skyline of Manhattan sped

by as the cab bounced over the bridge. She had no idea where they were going, but she was too intent on the conversation to notice. "If everyone just picked up whenever they felt like it and played hooky, the world wouldn't operate very smoothly," she observed, knowing that she sounded like a wet blanket.

Spencer laughed. "The world doesn't run very smoothly, anyway. I had jobs before, you know."

"You did?" She found that she was surprised. Somehow a mere job seemed too mundane for him. Jobs were for lesser mortals.

He nodded complacently. "Sure. But I didn't like any of them. And it wasn't because of the work. It was because I began to notice something."

"What?"

He watched the passing skyline for a moment and then continued. "The longer hours I worked, the less I saw of the bosses. When I was staying until six or seven at night, they were going home before rush hour."

She made a false cluck of sympathy. "Poor baby. And the sun was shining, there was a cloudless sky, and you were stuck inside a morgue, right?"

"As a matter of fact, yes. I remember one terrible heat wave. The thermometer was at ninety-five before it broke down. Then the air conditioner broke down." He laughed to himself. "And then I broke down. I got up and went right to the beach, all dressed up in my suit. I walked down to the water's edge and just kept going until I was drenched."

Emily pictured the outlandish sight and smiled. "What happened next?"

"I got a frantic call from the office. They offered to give me a raise and cut back on the hours if I would only come back. They were having trouble with a particular program that had just been created. The president of the firm told my boss that he'd be fired if the system wasn't fixed immediately, and I was the only one who could do it. So I simply charged them for the one job instead of returning to a salary. It took me three days to fix that computer, and I came away with a month's worth of salary. A good deal, don't you think?" Emily couldn't help but nod, fascinated. He shrugged, dismissing the rest of the story. "And I've been an independent consultant ever since."

"But . . . but you're just lucky," she sputtered. "Not everyone can do that."

"Why not?" he asked mildly.

"Independence is one thing," she continued, undaunted. "But you're mistaking freedom for license—license to do whatever pops into your head."

He shook his head firmly. "And you're mistaking blind, slavish devotion for loyalty and duty."

Emily said nothing, but her disapproval manifested itself in her stubborn frown. Maybe he thought she was just a stick-in-the-mud, but she had old-fashioned values and standards that had stood the test of time. Something about him didn't quite make sense—she had an inkling that there was an underlying conservatism hidden beneath his freewheeling façade—but his outspoken philosophy was completely contrary to everything she had been taught. He used his notion of freedom to escape real commitment and a sense of responsibility. It was all fine and well to talk about living independently; the results of such a life style were another matter.

She looked away as she realized that she could never get involved with a man like this. He was a troubleshooter, a rule breaker, and while such men were occasionally needed and had a place in the business world, they were quite foreign to her way of life.

Spencer McIntyre was a renegade, and for some unaccountable reason, that made her nervous. She felt vaguely that she shouldn't be here with him at all. He was exactly the sort of man her father would thoroughly disapprove of. She was her father's daughter, no doubt about that. McIntyre was definitely the odd man out. The thought of a meeting between the two men—as unlikely as it was—was a delicious one, making her smile unconsciously.

"I didn't know I was so amusing," Spencer said, breaking into her reverie.

"Oh, it's nothing," she answered. "I was just thinking about my father." Again the impish smile lit up her face, and she did nothing to conceal it from his alert eyes.

"Your father? Oh, the fellow with the jeep." She nodded, still smiling with a repressed secret. "Well, what about him?" he persisted.

"He'd tear you apart," she couldn't resist saying. "He'd eat you alive for breakfast and spit out the bones."

"Sounds very appetizing. Tell me more."

But Emily wasn't ready to do that. Not just yet, and maybe never. The more she thought about what she was doing in a cab with Spencer, the more she felt that she really should be going home. She had been introduced at the party as his associate, and while that had been a minor victory at the time, it no longer seemed appealing. Imagine, she scoffed to herself, living out of hotel rooms and moving from one city to the next. What a life! He must always eat in restaurants, she mused, and that reminded her of her present situation.

"Where are we going to eat?" she asked.

He smiled cordially, suddenly the gracious host. "You like Italian food?"

Emily nodded.

"I know a great little restaurant not too far from here. You'll love it."

"Sounds good," she allowed. "Where is it, in Queens?"

"Washington, D.C.," he answered nonchalantly.

Emily's mouth fell open as she stared at him, but he remained perfectly aloof, and she decided after a moment that he had only been teasing her. He wasn't exactly the most predictable person she had ever met. The cab continued to speed along the highway, and she found herself nettled at the flip remark.

"Can't you ever give a straight answer?"

He turned to her, genuinely surprised. "I did." He pointed at the road sign, nodding vigorously as the cab turned into the exit marked "La Guardia Airport." Emily watched in amazement as Al maneuvered the cab expertly toward the Eastern shuttle area, and she decided to put her foot down.

"Now wait just a minute," she said forcefully.

"What's the matter now?" Spencer asked. The cab pulled to a halt in front of the terminal, and he got out, waiting for her to join him. She refused to budge.

"I am not going to Washington with you," she announced flatly, still sitting in the cab. She glanced at her watch. "It's nine o'clock at night."

"So?" he asked impatiently. "What has that got to do with anything? We can be there in less than an hour. The restaurant isn't far from the airport. It's no big deal."

Emily was flabbergasted. She stared at him, the shock etched on her features. "I can't possibly do anything so rash," she said. "So extravagant."

"Extravagant?" He shrugged. "I do it all the time. People do commute, you know."

"Yes, but not like this. You couldn't have picked a restaurant in New York?" She saw that he was getting even more impatient with her, and it confounded her. *He* was getting impatient with *her*? The nerve of him!

"I have to get a few things out of my hotel room in Washington," he explained. "I thought we could kill two birds with one stone. I'll have you back in New York by one o'clock. Now, what do you say?"

Emily shook her head firmly and looked him squarely in the eye. "I say that you are a hopeless case, Spencer McIntyre. And a real nut." She leaned forward toward Al, who was waiting quietly for her to make up her mind. "Take me home," she commanded.

"Sure you won't change your mind?" Spencer asked calmly.

"I am very sure, thank you." She looked at him narrowly through the window. "And I'll tell you something else. I don't believe you're really going to Washington. I think it's all a part of your act."

"Act?" He blinked. "What act?"

"You know."

"I certainly don't."

"You're just trying to impress me in your own crazy way. No one goes to Washington just for dinner. You probably think you can sweep me off my feet by this jet-setter routine, but it's not going to work. I wasn't born yesterday, you know, in spite of your obvious need to believe that I was. You aren't going to trick me into your bed, Mr. McIntyre, so you might as well give up this act of yours."

Something very like anger flashed across his face, but he immediately backed off. "Very well," he said stiffly. "Have it your way. I assure you my intentions were perfectly honorable, madame, but I wouldn't dream of taking advantage of your famous virtue." He said all this mockingly, like a character in a play. "Besides," he added in his normal voice, "your virtue may not be as in demand as you think. I have no desire to seduce a high and mighty virgin."

Her eyes blazed and she sat up proudly. "I've had quite enough of this conversation," she announced with dignity. "Al, please take me home."

Spencer turned on his heel and walked into the terminal, and Al obediently pulled back onto the service road. They drove in silence for a minute until the cab was safely back onto the highway. Emily was embarrassed, knowing that Al and Spencer were friends. She knew that anything she said or did during the drive home would be reported back to Spencer. But Al surprised her.

"Wow," he said of his own accord.

"What do you mean?" she asked.

"I've never heard him talk to anyone that way. He really laced into you!"

Emily didn't know what to say to that, and she squirmed uncomfortably. "I really couldn't care less," she said. "Obviously, Mr. McIntyre doesn't think much of me, but that's quite all right with me, because I don't think much—"

"Noooo," he said expansively, cutting her off. "What're you talking about? I never heard him talk like that, never. He must really like you!"

Emily was speechless as the cab wound through the traffic toward Brooklyn.

Al deposited her in front of her apartment, and she thanked him and got out. "What do I owe you?" she asked.

"Nothing." He waved a hand in dismissal. "Spence takes care of it."

"I can pay my own way," she insisted. "How much is it?"

"I can't take it, lady. The boss would chew me out."

She relented reluctantly and fished for her key, walking up the steps to the front door. What a confusing evening it had been! Nothing could have prepared her for it, and she flattered herself that she had handled it all correctly. She sighed as she climbed the steps to her apartment and wearily brushed the short strands of hair out of her eyes. Suddenly, she felt very tired, even though it had actually been a short evening. Being with Spencer McIntyre was not conducive to relaxation.

She repressed a yawn as she opened her door, and she slipped out of her coat and threw it on a chair as she stepped inside. The wilted bouquet of flowers that she had found that morning was still sitting on the table where she had tossed it. She wondered fleetingly what had prompted it, but she had already had enough surprises for one night. Secret admirer notwithstanding, she wanted nothing more than to climb into bed early and get a good night's sleep. She kicked off her high-heeled black shoes, squirmed the zipper down the back of her dress, and stepped out of it. The dress had had a short-lived but highly effective night, she decided wryly. She wasn't sorry she had bought it; on the contrary, it had given her a new image and a new awareness of her own attractiveness. At least she had McIntyre and his annoying habit of challenging her to thank for that. The dress was stowed safely in the closet, and she padded into the bathroom in her underwear to wash up.

As she slipped a thin cotton nightgown over her head, the wilted bouquet of flowers again caught her eye. It looked so forlorn sitting limply on the table all by itself. She walked over to look at it, trying unsuccessfully to fluff the petals back into life. Then she noticed a thin, crisp envelope hidden behind a drooping blossom. She fished it out curiously and ripped it open, holding the enclosed message up to the light. There were two neatly printed lines on it, two very odd lines that seemed somehow familiar:

> *Just a note to let you know*
> *We're sorry we had to let you go.*
> —*F.I.I.*

She frowned, as if trying to nudge her memory. F.I.I. —Fenton International Industries, of course. Her former employer. Then it hit her like a thunderbolt.

Esmerelda! The computer! Her last night on the job at Fenton came back to her, the night in which she had whimsically, if pointlessly, programmed the computer to become Esmerelda. But maybe it hadn't been so pointless, after all. She remembered that she had instructed Esmerelda to send flowers and a note of condolence to all of the Fenton employees who had lost their jobs. And Esmerelda had obviously complied. But how? Why? She knew that she had discarded that tape, had heard it clang purposefully into the garbage before leaving. What had happened? Who had taken that tape and put it into the system? She didn't know.

Her mind fairly reeled with the possibilities and the consequences that were sure to follow. It was too late to track down the culprit. Whoever had picked up that tape had already done enough damage. What mattered now was that a multimillion-dollar industry was being disastrously affected by a harmless prank. Her heart sank as she recalled all of the crazy things she had taught the computer to do.

And of course that answered the question that had

been in the back of her mind all evening. She had wondered why Fenton needed a consultant and what had gone wrong that Spencer McIntyre, the world-renowned expert, couldn't fix. Well, now she knew. No one, not even a genius, would know how to undo a program that had been fancifully designed at her personal whim. It had had no particular code, no reason or method. It had been a one-shot, madcap spree, and she was the only person in the world who could possibly make any headway at correcting it.

Her heart beat faster as she wondered desperately if Spencer had known all along that she was the one who had caused the problem. There was no logical way for him to know, except that he was so brilliant and so perceptive that she believed he might know anything. She sighed tremulously as she considered the likelihood. He *must* know. Otherwise, why would he have picked her to be his assistant? Why would he have insisted so strenuously that she take the job? She was the only one who could help him, and he knew it.

He was right. And there was only one thing for her to do. She couldn't let her innocent practical joke turn into a nightmare. It wasn't fair. Even though she was still hurt that her job at Fenton had come to such an abrupt end, she couldn't let her personal feelings about the company interfere with what she knew was right. She would have to go back there and try to return the computer to some semblance of sanity.

Once her mind was made up, she wasted no time in taking action. She picked up the phone and called Spencer's hotel. The desk informed her that he wasn't in, and she wondered fleetingly where he was. Not that it was any of her business, of course. "Uh—I'd like to leave a message, please," she said. "A very important message. Yes. This is Emily Moreau." She spelled her

last name obligingly and continued the message.
"Please tell him that—I've changed my mind. I'll
take the job, after all." She waited as the message was repeated back to her. "That's right," she confirmed. "I'll start work first thing tomorrow morning."

Chapter Four

DATA REQUEST FROM EMPLOYEE #124-40-7434

Emily typed in the code word that would enable her to gain access to the computer's memory banks, hoping that the code would still be operative after her termination two weeks before. The terminal room was as empty as it had been the night she had left. It didn't look as if anyone at all had been there during the interim. The same gloomy silence permeated the atmosphere, broken only by the sounds of her fingers tapping lightly over the keys.

She hadn't wasted any time in getting there. It was only eight o'clock in the morning, and none of the other Fenton employees had arrived yet. She also hadn't heard anything from Spencer, but she hadn't expected to in so short a time. All she knew was that she wanted to get Esmerelda out of this computer as quickly as possible.

The machine digested her code, and she waited patiently for it to respond with the customary response of "Key Question." But what happened instead only increased her anxiety.

GOOD MORNING, EMILY, the computer responded. I HAVEN'T SEEN YOU SINCE YOU WERE TERMINATED. WELCOME BACK!

Emily blinked in amazement. Oh, no, she thought, this is worse than I thought. It was definitely her program, all right, but how had it found its way into the computer? She rubbed her eyes, fighting against the sleeplessness that had plagued her during the night. Once again, she approached the machine, armed with a new question.

LIST FUNCTIONAL DATA PRIOR TO—

She never completed the sentence. The computer neatly erased it and replaced it with a request of its own.

REQUEST INCOMPLETE—PLEASE REFER TO SERIES # 372-85 CODE WORDS PROPER ETIQUETTE.

Her hands trembling, Emily dutifully typed in a request for the etiquette requirements, the same etiquette she had programmed into this machine two weeks earlier. As she watched in awe, the computer listed all of the instructions she had given it on that fateful Friday. After studying the list briefly, she knew that she would have no trouble working with this computer, as quirky as it was. Her memory refreshed, her fingers flew along as she began her inquiry once again.

GOOD MORNING, ESMERELDA. WOULD YOU PLEASE LIST FOR ME ALL FUNCTIONAL DATA REFERRING TO PROGRAM CODED ESMERELDA.

She waited, expecting the computer to display the total scope of its new functions so that she would know where to begin. She wanted to know exactly how much control the computer had on the Fenton data banks. But what happened next was not part of her plan.

HAVE YOU HAD YOUR COFFEE YET? Esmerelda inquired.

Emily gaped in surprise. She didn't remember programming a coffee break. If she had been thinking clearly, she simply would have said yes, but the lack of sleep and sheer honesty caused her to automatically type in a negative response.

Esmerelda was not pleased. YOU WOULD FEEL A LOT BETTER IF YOU TOOK A TWENTY-MINUTE COFFEE BREAK. I'LL SEE YOU IN TWENTY MINUTES.

The screen went blank, and then a digital clock appeared, counting backward in minutes and seconds. Displayed above the clock were the words "Coffee Break."

Emily started to press the keys, anyway, hoping to continue her investigation, but nothing changed on the screen. No matter what she did, she couldn't break the code, and she threw up her hands in dismay.

This whole situation was unreal. But even Fenton and Spencer had agreed that the memory banks were still intact. The information was still there. It was the way in which the information had to be obtained that had changed. She had created a mechanical secretary, an electrical librarian that demanded polite behavior at all times. And to make matters worse, it now appeared to have its circuits intertwined with the personnel files, so that it could address each user personally. The threads of Esmerelda were interwoven throughout the tapestry of the company. To remove Esmerelda would be to remove whole segments of the system that were crucial to the working of the entire function. Although it was technically possible to get rid of Esmerelda and still leave the original system intact, it was highly unlikely that it could be done. It would be like playing a game of chess backwards, always trying to figure out which moves had come prior to the ones you were currently analyzing. It would be necessary to begin at the end of the game and work backwards until all of the pieces were set in their original positions.

The permutations were astronomical. One mistake and millions of bits of information would be destroyed. Emily sat watching the digital clock tick the countdown, wondering what to do. Did they know that she was the one who had wreaked this havoc? Or had Esmerelda provided her name as the most logical person to help Spencer? Esmerelda was smart enough to pick the very person who had created her. And yet Spencer McIntyre, even without the benefit of the data banks, was even smarter. As she sat there staring hopelessly at the screen, a hand extended a steaming mug of coffee in front of her.

"Spencer?" She straightened up immediately and turned around. He was dressed in jeans and a light blue shirt, just as he had been the first time she had seen him there. The tantalizing aroma of the coffee floated pleasantly by.

"Might as well take it," he said by way of greeting. "Esmerelda can get pretty huffy if you don't tell her the truth." Emily took the cup and looked back at the screen.

"Are you here on business or pleasure?" he asked with intended irony, quite unaware that her hand was shaking. She felt as if she had just been caught red-handed, but the feeling was irrational, and she brushed it aside. Steering the cup of coffee to her lips, she took a few sips and set it down. She still had ten minutes left before she could gain access to the computer again—if Esmerelda would let her.

"Business or pleasure?" Spencer repeated.

"Business," Emily said. "Strictly business."

He looked at the clock on the wall. "You're here awfully early. What's the big hurry?"

She was right. He *was* that smart. She would have to watch every step with him. "Curiosity," she replied smoothly. She tried a cool smile, but he only gave her a wry look.

"You ain't seen nothing yet," he informed her.

"Esmerelda is one smart cookie. It took me a week just to weed out all the coffee breaks she was giving everyone. She actually closed down three factories in Hong Kong five times a day. And in Detroit, she sent an entire staff of engineers home for the week, claiming that they were working around the clock and ruining their health." He chuckled and patted the top of the terminal fondly, as if it were a dog. "Actually, Esmerelda was right on the button. She ordered all of them to undergo physicals and wouldn't let them use the computer again until their medical data was programmed into her memory banks. And sure enough, two of the engineers were suffering from high blood pressure."

Emily was stunned.

"It's only the tip of the iceberg," he continued, making her turn pale. He pointed at the digital clock on the screen. "As I said, it took me a week to deprogram the coffee breaks, but the best I could come up with was a compromise. Whoever created this program was a genius. It's molded into every circuit it touches. Removing this program now will be like trying to remove the fruit from jello without breaking the mold."

Emily swallowed hard. He was absolutely right.

"I finally figured out how to play Esmerelda's game in order to effect a compromise." Emily looked up at him with frank admiration. Had he really figured out her program? If he had, he really was a genius. He had had no documentation to work with, nothing to study. The whole thing had been created at whim out of her head, and the only way to undo it would be to virtually read her mind. "It's like playing chess backwards," he added, startling her with the very same analogy she'd been thinking of herself. "Esmerelda's tentacles reach into the personnel files of every Fenton employee worldwide. Based on each person's individual history, she makes decisions as to how long and how hard they should work. So I made a deal with her."

"What kind of a deal?" Emily gulped.

"She can have the coffee breaks, but she had to give up prying into people's personnel records," he explained. He leaned against the wall, crossing his arms proudly. "She agreed to the compromise because I invented a simple formula that lets me negotiate with her. I taught her how to negotiate, and now she gives up some of her iron-fisted hold on production speed— when she thinks it's a fair deal."

Emily was astounded. Not only had he deciphered the intricacies of her program; he had invented one of his own that tied in effectively with hers. Spencer didn't know it, but he was now sharing a program with her. She was careful not to let him know that, however. All she said was "So, you gave Esmerelda one thing in order to get her to relinquish something else; is that it?"

"Precisely. And that's how I plan to continue, bit by bit, unless you can figure out a way to get rid of the old girl altogether. And frankly, I doubt that. If I couldn't do it, I really don't think it can be done." He spoke matter-of-factly, without arrogance.

Emily looked at him. "Why can't we get rid of her?"

"We can, but not without destroying three-quarters of all the valuable information in the memory banks that we want to keep." He walked over to her terminal and looked down at the computer with respect. "Esmerelda is immortal now. All we can do is to work with her, not against her. The next step is to get rid of the poet in her, and that's where you come in."

She almost jumped. "The poet? Oh, no. I don't believe this! The poet!" She looked at her screen and saw that her coffee break was over. Esmerelda would now allow her to gain access to the data banks.

"It seems our mystery programmer gave Esmerelda a cute little talent for spewing out information," Spencer said. "Go ahead, try it."

As Emily prepared to confront the computer once again, Vice-president Thompson stepped into the room. He was a youthful man, but highly conservative, always dressed in the correct corporate uniform. He was honest, straightforward, and very much a team player. He'd disapproved of the firing of the computer staff but had said nothing, not wanting to make waves. Emily recognized him because he was the one who had first hired her at Fenton, and she'd always liked him. It had been on his orders that she had been the last to go, but of course it was impossible to argue with a cold-hearted machine, and in the end he'd had to bow to the computer's demands. Now, as he saw whom McIntyre had brought in as his assistant, his face lit up in a pleased smile.

"So, Ms. Moreau," he said cordially. "You're the new troubleshooter in Mr. McIntyre's one-man operation." He turned to Spencer. "I must commend you on your choice. You picked a good employee."

"Associate," Spencer corrected him. "She works with me, not for me. This is a fifty-fifty partnership."

Thompson looked impressed. "That's very nice," he said evenly. "Tell me," he added in a more jovial tone, "is your name next to Mr. McIntyre's on his box at Grand Central Station? Or do you have a post-office box of your own?"

"The company is still called McIntyre, Inc.," Spencer answered for her. "Just address all correspondence to that."

Thompson nodded and then directed his attention to

Emily's terminal. "I'm expecting a potato shipment en route to the coast," he said, holding up a sheaf of papers and an invoice. "Do you think you could get the computer to tell me how long it will be before it arrives?" He placed the invoice next to the keyboard, and they watched as Emily obligingly began to enter the question into the computer.

INVOICE # 2245-POTATO.

Absolutely nothing happened.

"Oops," Emily said. "I know what I did wrong."

EXCUSE ME, ESMERELDA, she typed in.

YES? WHAT MAY I HELP YOU WITH? Esmerelda responded at once.

IF YOU'RE NOT TOO BUSY, WOULD YOU PLEASE LOCATE POTATO SHIPMENT # 2245?

I'D BE GLAD TO, EMILY. I HOPE YOU HAD A PLEASANT COFFEE BREAK.

The information appeared a second later, but Emily's face dropped in astonishment as she read the capricious way in which it was worded. As the three of them watched, Esmerelda furnished a most•unusual answer.


```
ONE POTATO, TWO POTATO, THREE POTATO, .
FOUR,
J. P. FENTON IS GOING TO BE SORE.
FIVE POTATO, SIX POTATO, SEVEN POTATO,
EIGHT,
THE SHIPMENT FROM BOISE IS THREE DAYS
LATE.
```


Emily was dumbstruck but managed a weak smile. She was relieved that the information was there at least, even in such an outlandish form. Thompson chuckled a little in spite of himself, but Spencer only stared impatiently at the screen.

"Well," Thompson said, clearing his throat, "I'll just leave you two to the task at hand." He headed toward the door and then stopped, turning back. "You know," he added as an afterthought, "in a way, I'll be sorry to see Esmerelda go. I must say, she's been a pleasant change around here. I actually think I'll miss her personality." He shrugged as if to say "too bad" and left.

Emily and Spencer were left alone. Suddenly, the silence between them seemed weighted, and she decided to let him be the one to speak first. He didn't say anything, though. He came up behind her, put his arms around her sides and typed quickly onto the keyboard.

ESMERELDA, PLEASE LIST ALL COMPUTER PERSONNEL BASED IN NEW YORK CITY AREA.

Immediately the screen flashed a list of seven names. Emily's was not among them.

"What's this for?" she asked.

"It's a list of all the people who had access to this computer last week," he explained. "One of them could have programmed a new system into the entire international complex."

"And you think one of them is guilty?" she asked, looking at the list without reading it.

Spencer shook his head and laughed. "This is only a list of suspects."

"You sound like Dick Tracy," she said dryly, but he only shrugged.

"It wouldn't matter even if we found him. It's too late."

Emily heard him say *him* and winced. But she felt a little better knowing that apparently no one suspected her. And of course she had not been the one to put the program into the computer. Someone else had been responsible for that. It had happened after she had left the company.

"Well," she said, sighing, "what's next on the agenda?"

His arms were still encircling her, and he made no effort to remove them. If she had been able to turn around, she would have seen the mischievous smile on his face, but she was imprisoned in his grasp. He said nothing, only drawing his arms closer around her until he had her locked in a hold from behind.

"What do you think you're doing?" she asked sternly. "How many times do I have to tell you, I don't mix business with pleasure."

He didn't budge. "So this is pleasurable?" he asked. "I thought so. Knock it off, Emily. You can't keep this up forever, you know. Besides, I suspect you want a little of both. Isn't that why you're here?"

"No," she answered weakly, keenly aware of his lean, muscled arms against her body.

"Then why are you here?"

She took a deep breath. "I'm here because—because—" She was stumped. How could she possibly tell him the truth now? "I'm here to fix the computer," she finished lamely.

"I don't understand you, Emily," he whispered into her ear. "Even Esmerelda has trouble with you."

She squirmed at the mention of Esmerelda. "What's that supposed to mean?"

He gave her a little squeeze. "She told me that you were a strange mixture of discipline and hidden energy just waiting for the right moment to escape. The question is How do I reach that part of you? Where is it? And how do I program my way into it?" He spoke with mesmerizing effect, letting the power of his words sink in. She said nothing, and he leaned forward, still holding her closely, and gently kissed her under her ear.

Emily sat immobile, too stunned to react, and he took advantage of her silence by continuing to leave tiny but fiery kisses all along the slender length of her neck. She knew she had to stop him, but some demon inside of her told her to wait just one more second so that she could prolong the delicious sensation. It was amazing that such a simple touch could fill her with such delight. The sheer intimacy of it shattered her composure, and she closed her eyes for a brief moment.

Much to her consternation, it was Spencer who stopped the stolen moment. "You see, Emily?" he asked in a low, persuasive tone. "You're fairly melting under my touch. That free spirit inside of you is bursting at the seams. I'm going to find it, and when I do, I'm going to capture it and let it loose."

She trembled and gripped her hands together. "Let go," she whispered, determined to regain her composure.

He did let go, but only to type another question into the computer.

PLEASE TELL ME HOW TO GET EMILY MOREAU TO GO OUT WITH ME FOR DINNER TONIGHT. He pressed the return key and she waited with a sinking heart to see what unorthodox reply Esmerelda would come up with this time. But Esmerelda had a little trouble.

PLEASE DEFINE PHRASE "GO OUT."

"You're wasting your time," Emily said. "She can't possibly understand—"

"Give her a chance," Spencer interrupted. He tried again.

PERSONNEL DATA CHECK, PLEASE. PLEASE LIST EMILY MOREAU'S FAVORITE FOODS.

Esmerelda went to work on that one, and a split second later the information was neatly constructed in a rhyme.

EMILY MOREAU IS A MERRY OLD SOUL,
AND A MERRY OLD SOUL IS SHE.
AND WHEN IT COMES TO DINNER TIME,
SHE LOVES FOOD FROM THE SEA.

Emily blanched, but Spencer beamed. "Perfect! I know a great place on Long Island. What do you say, Emily? Let's cut out early this afternoon and go for a swim before dinner."

She managed to turn around in her seat in order to give him a look that left no doubt as to her reaction. "Out of the question," she said. "And, anyway, we have far too much work to do."

"I can see you're going to be difficult about this." He sighed, abruptly removing his arms and stepping back.

She stared at him, trying to look stern, but inside she was frantically trying to deny that she was sorry he had released his grasp.

He didn't see her inner turmoil. "Okay, okay," he relented. "All work and no play, all right?"

She nodded wordlessly. What kind of a man was he, she wondered, still staring at him. There they were, on an important job, and all he wanted to do was to go to the beach.

As if he had read her thoughts, he said, "Well, Emily, if it's all work and no play today, then I think I'll just sign off and go to the beach today."

Her mouth fell open in surprise. "But—but what about this job?"

"What about it?"

"You can't just walk out! This could easily take all week," she sputtered. "What is the matter with you? Don't you have any sense of responsibility at all?"

"I've been here two weeks," he countered, "and I've barely made any headway with Esmerelda at all. What difference is an afternoon going to make? I need a break. I'm not going to get anything done today. My mind needs a rest."

"Oh. Well, I'll stay here, and you can go and . . . take a break. But no dinner tonight—or any night."

He smiled in that mischievous way she was coming to know all too well. "Rank and file to the end, eh?"

She refused to be swayed. "Something like that," she said seriously.

"God and company."

Emily smiled. It was her turn to take control as she remembered her new status. "Don't forget, McIntyre," she said, "we're partners now. If one of us fails at something, we're both to blame. So scoot," she finished, waving him off airily. "I'll give this the old army try."

"Yes, ma'am," he said, giving a mock salute. Then he relaxed his stance and gave her a baleful grin. "But you still have to eat, you know. We could take a late break and—"

"OUT!" she commanded, pointing at the door. "March!"

Much to her surprise, he burst out laughing. Not only did he ignore her command, but he came up behind her and gave her a hug that was unmistakably affectionate. "Emily!" he cried. "Now that's a new part of you that I haven't seen before." He laughed again, obviously enjoying himself. "You're not merely good at taking orders—you're very good at giving them! I should have known." He shook his head ruefully and gave her another deliberate squeeze before backing off. "Just remember one thing, though, sergeant." His tone became suddenly serious. "In this company, I'm still chairman of the board."

She shrugged and pointed once again at the door. "Take the rest of the day off, Mr. Chairman. I have work to do."

He turned on his heel and left without another word. She sat and listened to his footsteps as he walked briskly to the elevator. The doors banged with a definitive sound, and Spencer McIntyre was off to the beach.

Emily found that she was somewhat relieved. She really did want to make some sense out of the confusion she had created in Esmerelda, and she couldn't do that with Spencer always hanging over her shoulder . . . and holding her in his arms. She brushed the memory of his touch aside and concentrated on the screen in front of her. It was no time to start mooning like a schoolgirl.

She sat quietly for a few minutes, trying to decide how to go about her task. Finally, she decided that it would be best to try to recreate her program from scratch. The only way to do it was from memory. She began resolutely, determined to stretch her recollection as far as she could, and hour after hour went by as she continued the arduous chore of duplicating a complex system that she had invented two weeks before. By the time she was finished, it was nearly two in the afternoon.

No one had bothered her; no one had interrupted her or even noticed her sitting there so dutifully. She'd expected to see Thompson again, or maybe even Fenton, but the terminal room had been invaded only by a few stragglers who came around to check on basic operations. It was extremely isolating, and she realized with a start that she'd missed Spencer and his antics.

He was beginning to grow on her, and she had no idea how she was going to handle it. But she was saved temporarily by the sense of duty that had kept her chained to the terminal all day long, and she entered the final bits of information doggedly, determined to complete the task thoroughly. Esmerelda, however, had something else in mind.

HAVE YOU HAD YOUR COFFEE BREAK THIS AFTERNOON? Emily pursed her lips, and quickly typed in, YES, I HAVE.

But Esmerelda was too clever for her. "YOU'RE NOT TELLING THE TRUTH, EMILY. YOU DIDN'T EVEN STOP FOR LUNCH. Suddenly, the screen went blank. A digital clock appeared, this time counting off a whole sixty minutes, and the words "Lunch Break" flashed on top of the screen.

"Damn!" Emily cried, punching the terminal in frustration. But there was nothing she could do about it. Esmerelda had the upper hand. Realizing that it was useless to argue, Emily got up, stretched and headed out of the building for lunch. She had to admit that Esmerelda had a point. She'd been working all day, and she was hungry.

Outside, the hot, muggy street offered no relief. The sun beat down, reflecting mercilessly off the buildings, and Emily trudged dispiritedly to a sandwich shop where she grabbed a quick bite. Even as she munched it, her mind was racing with formulas and permutations as she searched for some combination that would get Esmerelda to relinquish her control of the data banks. It was astounding that Spencer had been able to make any progress at all. She had to admit he was brilliant. If only he weren't so aggressive, as well.

His nearness had been disturbing. It had awakened feelings in her that were supposed to remain dormant during business hours, and it fascinated her and frightened her that she'd been unable to control them. She didn't know how much longer she would be able to face him with a cool and professional attitude. The man was definitely getting to her, and he knew it. But she had to stay on the job. She felt driven to do as much as she humanly could to fix what she had done as quickly as possible. Spencer McIntyre and his devilish gray eyes notwithstanding, she had a responsibility.

The clock on the wall told her that the hour was up, and she wasted no time in wending her way back through the oppressive heat. Thankfully, the Fenton Building was air conditioned, and she entered the doors with a distinct sense of relief. She was glad now that Esmerelda had insisted she go for lunch. Armed with new energy and a second wind, she worked straight into the early evening. Twice Esmerelda told her to go home, but artfully using Spencer's tactics with logical negotiation, she managed to bargain for an extra four hours. But by ten o'clock Esmerelda was tired of negotiations.

GO HOME, EMILY. YOU'RE EXHAUSTED. I'LL SEE YOU TOMORROW.

Emily stared at the words on the screen, and for once she decided not to give Esmerelda an argument. She *was* exhausted. Her mind was reeling from all the painstaking work she had done, and she couldn't even close her eyes without seeing tiny, computerized green letters flying by. Slowly, she stood up, turning off the computer and switching off the lights. She felt limp as she walked down the deserted corridor.

Downstairs in the lobby, she signed out of the building and headed through the double doors. The street was quiet at that time of night, but she was relieved and happy to see Al sitting in his cab, waiting for her. She waved at him, and he motioned for her to get in. She sank back gratefully against the seat, wondering what on earth Spencer had been doing all day.

Spencer didn't show up at all the next day, and she didn't try to find him. She was too busy trying to get Esmerelda out of the computer. But the longer she worked, the more frustrated she became. The job was hideously tedious, requiring infinite patience and perseverance. And she made practically no progress at all. Once again she worked straight through the day, stopping only when Esmerelda forced her to, and she was still there long after everyone else in the company had gone home. It was almost like her old days at Fenton except that this time there was no one to keep her company and nothing to provide any encouragement. The hours ticked by until at last she fell across the terminal, utterly exhausted and driven to despair.

"Forget it. Esmerelda can't be removed."

The words filtered slowly through her mind, and very reluctantly, she opened her eyes. "What . . . ?" she mumbled.

It was Spencer. He was staring down at her, looking his usual jaunty self, and her hand flew self-consciously to her face.

"What—what time is it?" she croaked, stifling a yawn as she tried to smooth her hair into place.

His face changed as something dawned on him. "Good Lord," he exclaimed. "Don't tell me you slept here all night!" He threw her another glance and then walked over to the electric coffeepot and plugged it in. "I've been trying to reach you all night," he said. "Al called me and said you must have left work early yesterday, because he waited outside for you, but you never showed up. He figured you must have left before he got there." He shook his head disapprovingly. "Now I see why you never went home in his cab last night. You never even made it out of the building."

She sat up slowly, trying to look less tired than she was. "I must have fallen asleep over the terminal," she said, looking around at the all-too-familiar room. Her eyes came to rest on Spencer's lean, merry face. "You look fine," she observed tartly. "In fact, you've got yourself one heck of a tan."

"And you look as pale as a ghost. Just how long were you at this, anyway?" He held up a hand to stop her from answering. "Don't bother to answer. I'll get the information from a more reliable source." He went over to the terminal and keyed in the question. Esmerelda took no time at all to respond.

```
EMILY MOREAU WORKS ROUND THE CLOCK,
TICKETY TOCK, TICKETY TOCK.
TWENTY-THREE HOURS IN JUST TWO DAYS,
LATE INTO THE NIGHT SHE STAYS.
```

The screen then went blank, but Esmerelda came back with a new message.

```
ALL WORK AND NO PLAY MAKES EMILY A DULL
GIRL.
TAKE A VACATION, GO ON A WHIRL.
```

The screen went blank again and stayed that way. Emily threw her hands up. "She's sending me home again! I don't believe it!"

The sound of Spencer's laughter cut her short, and

she wheeled around angrily to face him. "This is not funny!"

"Yes, it is," he said, grinning. "Esmerelda is right, you know. She usually is. It's what I've been telling you all along."

"What?" she said fiercely. "That I'm a 'dull girl'?"

He nodded complacently. "Only on the surface. And that's your own doing."

"Well, it's none of your business!" she snapped. She was getting tired of his challenging her like this. It wasn't fair.

"Take it easy, Emily," he said in the same maddeningly calm voice. "I just spent the last two days dreaming up new programs on the sand at low tide." He smiled ironically. "Jones Beach is very conducive to that sort of thing. And I'm positive that we can't take Esmerelda out of this computer—ever."

"We have to!" she said adamantly.

Spencer gave her a shrewd look and poured her a cup of coffee. "Why is it so important to you?" He handed her the coffee.

"How can you just give up?" she countered, avoiding his question.

"Easily. When something can't be done, I don't waste my time. I have other jobs waiting."

She looked at her lap. "Well, I won't quit," she said stubbornly.

He came up behind her, and before she could stop him, his hands were on her shoulders, gently but firmly massaging. His touch was exquisitely soothing. He rubbed and cajoled her tired muscles, and when her nerve endings were tingling with satisfaction, he stroked the sensitive skin at the back of her neck until the thread of desire that had been smoldering beneath leaped into flames. Emily closed her eyes against the tender assault. She was tired and frustrated and wor-

ried, and she wanted nothing more than to shut out the
world by surrendering her senses to this persuasive fire.
She had been fighting him ever since she had met him,
and suddenly she didn't know why. He was so carefree,
so impossibly independent . . . and so devastatingly
attractive. Her head fell back, and the graceful gesture
of surrender ironically made her open her eyes.

"How long will it take you to go home and change
into a bathing suit?" he asked in velvety tones.

She blinked in surprise and straightened up hastily.
The screen flashed the words "Take the day off, Emily"
in iridescent green.

"Are you always so direct?" she whispered.

Spencer chuckled. "Not always. Sometimes I resort
to down and out subterfuge."

She managed a smile. "What makes you think I was
talking to you?"

As she changed and waited for Spencer to pick her
up, Emily thought about everything that had happened. She didn't know why she was going to the beach
with him, of all places, but her father had always
maintained that actions speak louder than words. If she
was going to the beach, it meant that she was willing to
let something happen between them. And she wanted it
to. She wasn't sure what she would do once it started.
She might even decide against further involvement in
the end. But his teasing and goading had challenged her
such that she had to prove to both of them that she
wasn't afraid. It was time to stop hiding. She put her
mind on automatic pilot as she straightened her apartment and sorted quickly through the mail that had
come in the last few days. There was nothing unusual—
just the regular array of bills and ads. But one letter did
catch her attention. She ripped it open as soon as she
saw it, grinning even before its contents were revealed.

"Em," it said. "I'll be on two weeks' leave starting next week. Keep your schedule open and don't make any fancy plans. Over and out. All my love, Stretch."

Emily tossed the letter on the kitchen counter and checked her wall calendar. Then she remembered that her schedule consisted only of Esmerelda—and Spencer McIntyre. Something told her that there were now two men in her life, and it would be a distinctly bad idea for them to cross paths. Two more opposite men would be hard to find.

The doorbell interrupted her thoughts. She found herself running to answer it and consciously slowed down, adopting a neutral expression. But when she opened it, she got an unexpected surprise.

"My God!" she gasped. "What happened to you?"

"We had a little accident on the Brooklyn Bridge," Spencer answered. He looked dizzy, and his left eye was adorned with a black and blue mark.

"A little accident? It looks like you practically went through the windshield."

Al came up the steps behind him, looking winded. "It was a near miss," he admitted. "Mind if I wash up?"

She let them both in and took Spencer firmly by the arm. "Come with me," she ordered, leading him into the kitchen. She quickly prepared an ice pack and handed it to him. "Was anyone else hurt?" she asked as he applied it carefully to his eye.

Al's loud laughter could be heard from inside the bathroom.

"Why is that funny?" she demanded. Anything was possible with these two characters.

"I'm not laughing, am I?" Spencer asked grimly. He sat down at the kitchen table as Al entered the room.

"I told you, Spence," Al said. "You should have let me do the talking." He turned to Emily to explain. "He got a broadside by a real old pro. I saw it coming, but I wasn't fast enough to stop it. That old guy sure had quick reflexes, though. I wouldn't want to tangle with him, I can tell you that."

Emily was completely perplexed. "What in thunder are you talking about?" She sat down next to Spencer and peeked at his eye. He said nothing, so she looked at Al, who was also silent. She kept looking back and forth between the two of them—one with the black eye and the other with the florid, reddish face. "Would one of you mind telling me what happened?" she asked quietly.

Spencer lifted a hand and waved it weakly toward Al.

"Who, me?" Al said. "Well, I was just driving along when this official-looking car cuts me off on the bridge. Spence saw the whole thing, didn't you, Spence?" He was gathering steam, but Spencer only nodded stonily. "It wasn't my fault at all. This guy shaved off my right fender, not to mention half the door right where Spence was sitting. I thought it was all over for a second. So I pulled over and got out. A young kid was driving the other car."

"And he punched Spencer in the eye?" She looked at Spencer and winced. "Why? What did you say to him?"

"Very little," Al said emphatically, continuing the story. "Spencer suggested that we all drive over the bridge and meet on the other side to exchange insurance and all of that. All the traffic was backing up, and people were honking like crazy. So the next thing I know, this old coot—" He turned to Spencer for confirmation. "That's what you called him, right?"

Spencer nodded unenthusiastically. "That's what he was."

"Yeah. Well, this old coot jumps out of the back seat of the other car and starts ordering everyone around.

He said I drove like a real New Yorker. He just wouldn't shut up. Well, I don't like being insulted, naturally, but I couldn't get a word in, and the cars were backed up all the way across the bridge. I couldn't believe it. So Spencer here says—"

Spencer sighed and gingerly removed the ice pack from his eye. "I said, 'Listen, you old coot. If you don't get back in that car and get off this bridge, I'm going to toss you into the river.' But he wouldn't listen. He just kept right on yelling at everybody, and finally I put up my hand to try and get his attention. He was really bugging me."

"The next thing I know, the old guy's right hook is slamming into Spence's eye. What a temper! Spence never even saw it coming."

Spencer shook his head ruefully. "When my head stopped spinning, the old coot was back in his car, driving off."

"I got his license number, though," Al said proudly. "When we catch him, he'll be in for it. You should see what my cab looks like."

Spencer said nothing, putting the ice pack on his eye again, and Emily waited for Al to continue. The story seemed to be at an end, however, and at length she said, "Uh—does this mean we're not going to the beach? I don't mean to sound disinterested in your adventure, but if we're not going, I think I'll change."

"Of course we can go," Al said stoutly. "I need a day on the beach more than ever after that. This heat wave is driving me nuts. Let's go."

"Ohhh!" Spencer groaned. "Don't you two have any consideration? How can you be so hedonistic when my head is splitting open?"

Al and Emily exchanged glances. "Is he serious?" she asked.

"No," Al answered jovially. "He just likes sympathy." Spencer gave him a baleful glare, groaned loudly and drew himself slowly to his feet.

"Come on," Emily encouraged him. "You'll feel better if you stop worrying so much and just go to the beach. The ocean breeze will be good for you.

Spencer's face lit up in a broad smile. "That's just what I was waiting to hear you say."

Emily's face dropped, but Al only looked at him patiently. "Did you remember to bring your pail and shovel?" he asked.

Spencer grinned. "Of course." He held up a plastic bag. "Let's go."

"I have never seen a grown man with so many toys," Emily commented as the three of them made their way across the white sand toward the ocean shore. The delicate scent of salt water and the fresh, persistent breeze were already revitalizing her. The days of slavish work receded magically into the background.

Spencer was carrying an odd assortment of tools. Two blue and red plastic pails were tucked under his arm, filled with a large butter knife, a soup spoon, a small shovel, various cookie-cutter molds, and a large round board decorated with a picture of a surfer riding the waves.

"What's that thing?" she asked, pointing at the disc.

"What, this?" He held it up. "It's a skim board. You ride it at low tide on an inch or less of water."

She didn't know if he was teasing her or not, so she stole a glance at Al. "Where did you find him?" she asked.

Al wasn't playing. "Hey, Spence," he said. "When you're not using it, can I play with it?"

"Sure, Al. But be careful with it. Don't let any of the kids on the beach wheedle you into giving them a ride."

Emily decided to ignore them. She threw her blanket down on the sand and smoothed out the edges. "I'm parking myself right here," she announced. "You two can go play hide-and-seek if you like, but I'm going to concentrate on getting a tan." She plopped down on the blanket and lifted her T-shirt over her head, revealing the cleverly cut top of a red bikini. Both Spencer and Al were staring at her frankly, and she stopped for a moment, reluctant to go on. But this was a beach, and it was ridiculous to assume sudden modesty. She slowly drew her cotton pants down her slender legs and kicked them aside, drawing her knees up to her chest.

"On second thought," Spencer announced, "I think I'll stay here and forego the toys." Al had the grace not to smile, and Spencer sat down next to her, lifting his own shirt over his head. It was Emily's turn to stare candidly, and she did. His chest was lean but nicely muscled, already sporting a bronze tint, and he moved carelessly, with masculine grace. His jeans followed, revealing a pair of black bathing trunks that were molded tightly around his narrow but powerful hips. Emily put her chin on her knees, her large eyes like saucers as she gave him a sidelong stare.

"Come on, Emily," he said suddenly. "I'll teach you how to ride on the ocean."

Before she could protest, he grabbed her hand and pulled her up, dragging her down to the water. The tiny bikini top barely covered her breasts as she ran along, and she peeked down to make sure that they were still hidden beneath the red fabric. She had never worn anything that revealing. The black dress had been the beginning of a spree that she was somehow unable to contain. It had something to do with showing Spencer that she wasn't the square he seemed to think she was, but as she ran down to the water, feeling like an ad for a

California soft drink, she wondered if she hadn't carried her reaction too far.

The cold water washed up to touch their toes, and Spencer threw the large disc onto the sand. "What is that thing?" she asked. "A Frisbee?"

"No. Watch." He picked it up again and waited until a large, rolling wave came into shore. The moment it began to retreat, he threw the disc onto the remaining inch of water and jumped onto it, skimming the beach as he balanced on the lightweight board. He traveled along for several yards, his long, lean legs bracing and flexing to keep him afloat. At length, he jumped off again, his face shining with merriment. "Now it's your turn," he announced.

"Oh, no. I'll fall off."

"No, you won't. Come on." He grabbed her hand again and led her closer to the water. "I'll run alongside you so you won't fall," he said. Emily wasn't sure how she felt about that arrangement, but she didn't have much time to think about it. Without warning, another wave crashed around their feet and Spencer pulled her sideways down the beach where the skim board was just grazing the water. "Jump!" he shouted, and she did, landing squarely on the board and instinctively keeping her balance with her arms.

She realized dimly that the shriek of delight was her own and that Spencer was running next to her, his arm braced protectively in back of her. She was being propelled along the water's edge like a water skier, until at last the wash of water ended. She was about to gracefully jump off again, but Spencer pulled her right into the water, hooting and splashing as they were assailed by another wave that plastered their hair to their heads. The cold, bracing water was exhilarating. Emily emerged for air, laughing and diving under the water again like a seal. She felt completely refreshed and invigorated, the hot day and her skimpy bathing suit forgotten. The sun shone gloriously down on the beach, and suddenly she had all the energy in the world.

"That was fun!" she called. "Let's do it again!"

"Not now," he said, swimming toward her. "Maybe later." He threw the skim board onto the beach, where it was retrieved by Al and a group of kids who had been hovering nearby. He turned in the water to face the ocean, waiting for the next wave. Emily looked around and saw that everyone in the water was doing the same thing. When it came, it was a small one, and they all were pushed up gently for a moment off the ocean floor. Emily landed again with a slight bump.

Spencer was still scanning the ocean for a good wave, and she looked at him solicitously. "You'd better be careful," she said. "That eye could still make you dizzy."

"Don't worry about me," he said, floating closer to her. He slid an arm around her waist and held her as another small wave bumped them gently up. She lost her footing for a moment and was pushed against him. Her breasts squashed against his chest, and he was obliged to hold her so that she wouldn't fall. When the wave passed and her feet found the ocean floor again, he kept holding on to her, his strong arms pinning her in his grasp.

The powerful movement of the current swept between their legs so that her legs slid against his. She could feel all the hard, lean lines of him, and the softness of her body molded for one brief second to his masculine contours. Something in him seemed to change, and somehow she felt a change also stealing over her. She had been trying to deny that Spencer was a powerfully attractive man and that she was a very vulnerable young woman. Now, suddenly, her denial seemed ridiculous. It felt so natural and easy to be standing there with him like that, half covered by the Atlantic Ocean. Esmerelda was far, far away. There was nothing but sun and sand and sea—and a man who had come so effortlessly and irrevocably into her life.

But the heady moment was interrupted as a giant wave came crashing down on them. Spencer had been looking down with a gentle but demanding expression into her eyes, and for a second it had been as if they were all alone out there in the water. When the water cascaded over them, they were both toppled headlong into its midst and washed with driving force onto the shore. Emily's head was spinning, and for a few glorious seconds her world consisted of nothing but the salt water that enveloped her. She was flung like a missile toward the shore, deliciously helpless to struggle against the power of the water. But the wave subsided as quickly as it had come, and she was able to find her footing in the shallow water. Spencer poked his head out of the water just as she was gasping for breath, and they both laughed uproariously.

They swam back out, waiting for another wave. This time they were prepared for it, and when it was just behind them, they dove ahead of it and let it carry them in. Once again, Emily was caught in the watery whirlwind that left her senses reeling. Spencer swam back out while she shook the water from her eyes, and just as she prepared to join him, he was hurtling toward her like a torpedo. He knocked her down, so that both of them were sprawled in the shallow water, the rhythmic motion of the wave washing over their legs.

"You don't quit, do you?" she said breathlessly.

"What do you mean?" he asked in mock protest. "You're the one who doesn't quit, remember?"

But she didn't want to remember. She didn't want to think about anything except that moment, and she continued to sit in the water, her legs bent at the knee. Her smile was mischievous as she said, "Maybe there's a lot you don't know about me."

"I already know that. I told you as much the first day I met you. You've got surprises hidden under that cool exterior, even when you're only covered by that bathing suit." His eyes traveled frankly over her curves, and she scooped up a handful of water and tossed it at him.

"Careful," he warned. "I'm a champion dunker."

"I'm sure you are," she said serenely. "But first you'll have to catch me." With that, she threw herself toward the deeper water, swimming forcefully out to sea. Spencer dove in after her, and his powerful strokes soon brought him to her side. They stood on a small mound, bouncing up and down in the smaller waves, laughing out of breath. He looked as happy as a child in that setting. It was as if the beach were a magical world for him in which he could rid himself of daily cares and let go. He enjoyed everything to its fullest extent, living from moment to moment. She had to struggle to keep up with his energetic zeal. He couldn't get enough of life, as if it were his last day on earth and he was driven to capture every single second of it. She looked at him with a new kind of respect. His gray eyes were gleaming, reflecting the long rays of the sun, and he mastered the swell of the waves easily, letting them pass him by as they raced into shore.

Suddenly, he noticed her staring at him, and she tried to look away. But he caught her chin in his hand and stared solemnly back at her until at last they seemed to be the only two people there, alone in the Atlantic Ocean. A single line seemed to flow between them, linking and anchoring them together on its invisible length. They came together wordlessly, drawn by the powerful feeling, and in an instant his strong arms were pulling her close. Their mouths met, longingly at first, and then with fiery ardor as his tongue found hers and teased it into honeyed battle.

The rhythmic motion of the incoming waves rocked them to and fro, and Emily clung to him, drinking in the sweetness of the kiss. She opened for him like a flower, her senses reeling as she lost herself in the swirling sensation. They stood there together, entwined in their own private world, until a large wave splashed their shoulders and sent them floating onto their backs.

"Let's go in," Spencer said, and she nodded breathlessly, her eyes still glowing from the impact of the kiss. They paddled in slowly, not looking at each other, but when they reached the shallow water and stood up, Spencer firmly imprisoned her hand in his, and they walked together back to her blanket.

"Look at all the people here," she commented, wanting to break the silence. "It seems like a lot—for a weekday, I mean. You'd think—"

"That they should all be at their jobs working," he finished for her. "Right?" He smiled. "I'll bet half of these people called in sick today just to have an excuse to go to the beach." He picked up a towel and vigorously rubbed it on his arms and his chest. "Don't you understand, Emily? It's okay to escape once in a while. We all need it sometimes. It's just that some people are too rigid—"

"Or maybe just responsible," she interjected.

"Rank and file," he said, shaking his head. "Always rank and file. Think about it, Emily. Do most people really put in an eight-hour workday? Don't they stretch their coffee breaks, come in at nine-thirty instead of nine, take a little extra on their lunch hour and spend time gossiping by the water cooler?"

"The world of Spencer McIntyre," she said grandly. "If it feels good, do it."

"Not quite." His tone was almost stern, and it surprised her.

"Well, you didn't get rich lying around on the beach," she insisted.

"No." Then he smiled. "But there were times when I spent all of my working hours on the beach. Watch." He knelt down in the sand and found a stone with a sharp edge. As Emily stared, he began to make notations in the hard sand. She saw that he was writing a series of simple formulas, labeled Esmerelda, Culprit and McIntyre. She continued to watch with avid interest as he listed the latest series of commands that she herself had just finished working on. They paralleled what she had achieved almost exactly.

"When did you have time to do all of that?" she asked in astonishment. But she already knew the answer. "This is certainly a great place to work," she admitted. "You've got the whole beach for a blackboard."

He continued making notations, moving closer to the water. "Now here's our culprit's main line of thought," he explained, writing quickly. "Every programmer has a style all his own. It's like writing a book or painting a picture. Each style is unique. He gave her a sidelong grin. "Most people think that computer programming is anything but creative, but you and I know better."

"That's true," she allowed.

"Believe me, I've seen hundreds of programs that were logically and functionally the same, but stylistically, they were completely different."

"And so now you know the culprit's style?" she asked fearfully.

"I know more than that." They watched as a long wave came up and washed away a part of what he had written. "I now understand something about our culprit, something about his personality. It took me a few days of sitting out here and working in the sand, but it was worth it. I figured out not only that we were wasting our time trying to deprogram Esmerelda but that our culprit may not have had any intention of putting that program into the computer in the first place. It could have been an accident—a very unusual one, but an accident nonetheless.

A rush of relief spread over her. She was sorely tempted to tell him the truth—all of it—but something held her in check.

"Look here," Spencer said, pointing to a series of commands that she easily recognized. "That's the sequence that was used to give Esmerelda her manners."

"Oh—the etiquette."

"Yes. And it was very difficult to do." He looked up and smiled. "That is, it would have been unless the programmer was thoroughly familiar with the complex system of the company."

"And only seven people were," she said brightly. "The remaining New York staff."

"Wrong," he responded in the same cheerful voice, making her heart sink. "There were twenty-nine specialists in the New York office before seventy-five percent of them were fired. Our culprit could be any one of them."

"But—but Esmerelda wasn't activated until after they were fired."

"I know." He nodded. "That's why I think it may have been an accident. I reviewed the backgrounds of the seven remaining people, and to put it simply, none of them has the brains to write up a program as complex as this one. Fenton doesn't know it, but he fired a very rare individual with an extraordinary talent."

"Oh."

"Not to mention a very rare and unique sense of

humor," he added. He started laughing. "You know something, Emily? If I ever decide to expand my business, I think I'd like to hire this character. He's just what I need to add some spunk to this industry."

"Spunk!" She tried to look disapproving. "But what's so important about spunk?"

"Everything," he said seriously. "That guy must be laughing his head off right now, knowing that we can't get Esmerelda out of the computer, no matter what we do. It's as though he left a nice chunk of his personality inside that computer."

"Really?" She knew she was sounding a little dense, but he was too eager to impart his theories to notice.

"Sure. That's part of his style. He unconsciously put his own feelings into the system. And starting next week, I'm going to begin reviewing the styles of all twenty-seven people until I find the same fingerprint that makes Esmerelda so unique. Then I'm going to call up the guy and see if he's interested in working with me."

Emily looked away. He had already called her his associate, but apparently he hadn't been serious. And yet he was willing to offer a partnership to some stranger, someone he'd never even met. An odd little smile crossed her face as she thought about it. Little did he know that this talented and unusual "guy" was sitting right next to him on the beach.

The tide was coming in slowly, and each new wave wiped away more and more of Spencer's scribblings in the sand. So this was what he had been doing all week. He had taken his work with him in his head in order to play Sherlock Holmes. What he didn't know was that it was his own Watson he was closing in on. Once again she was very tempted to tell him everything, but again she decided against it. She had no idea how he would take it, and she didn't want to spoil anything about that day. But it seemed inevitable that he would figure it out eventually. She was aghast at how much he had figured out already.

"Uh—I think I'll take a little nap," she said. She needed time to think.

"What? Oh, sure. Go ahead. You've been working too hard. You can use the rest. We won't talk about work anymore today. Don't forget, Esmerelda gave strict orders for you to take the day off. And you know what an uncanny way she has of finding out if you've been telling the truth."

She smiled a little. "That's true."

He picked up his pail and shovel and other paraphernalia. "It's sand-castle time for me."

"Enjoy yourself," she said. "I think my sand-castle days are long gone."

"Not mine," he answered, and ran down to the water, tools in hand.

She lay back on the blanket, but sleep eluded her. The image of Spencer McIntyre kept racing through her mind, and she struggled to make sense out of his contradictions. He seemed to have no sense of responsibility, and yet he had spent the last few days feverishly working out formulas on this beach. Finally, she sat up and squinted through the sun to look at him. He was happily involved with the construction of a sand castle, like a kid without a care in the world. He was only about ten feet from the water's edge, and soon the tide would reach him. That was Spencer, she thought ruefully. Building something fleeting—like his life. Here one day and gone the next. Living out of hotel rooms and eating in offbeat restaurants.

What kind of a life was that? After six years, it seemed that he would want a home of his own, and a— She caught herself short. But the thought had surfaced and refused to go away. A wife. It seemed that by now, he would want a wife. She told herself that it was none of her business, that his personal life was nothing to her. But her traitorous imagination immediately went on a tangent, conjuring up a picture of what it would be like to be married to him. He was such a nomad. How could he ever hope to have a family or establish roots? No, he wasn't exactly the sort of man a girl would want to bring home and introduce to her dad. The idea of her father made her smirk.

Emily turned over and flopped onto her stomach. Spencer was busily building a wall of sand, piling it higher and higher and forming a small moat in front of it. She watched the water rushing toward the shore and realized that he meant to use the tide to fill the moat. Very logical, she had to admit. And yet it was baffling. Spencer was never what he appeared to be at first glance.

As he worked diligently, a contented smile crept onto his face and stayed there. She had never seen anyone so absorbed. A little girl in a pink bathing suit wandered over to watch him, and Emily smiled. The girl was about four or five, and she carried her own pail and shovel. She stood there for several minutes, watching him at work, and finally he looked up and noticed her. He said something to her, and she responded shyly. Then she sat down next to him in the sand, and to Emily's surprise, she began to pile more sand on the wall. They continued to work together in harmony, constructing a bridge and another wall, and after a while, Emily fell into a light doze.

When she awoke, she had no idea how much time had passed, but the sun was still hot, and the wind had picked up a little. She lifted her head and squinted down the beach to see how the sand castle was progressing and discovered to her amazement that Spencer was now surrounded by a whole group of small helpers.

The simple castle wall had grown into a huge complex with various levels, designs and towers. The ocean was closer by at least five feet, and a little bit of water was beginning to seep into the moat. She watched as he began explaining where the castle would expand, and the children listened enthusiastically and carried out his directions. It was an extraordinary sight. Emily reflected that if he could manage people as well as that, he could have quite a business. After a few more minutes, she lazily stretched and stood up and walked down to the shore to join the group.

Spencer looked up with a happy smile. "We're building King Arthur's castle," he said. "In another ten minutes, the evil wizard will send the forces of the ocean to destroy the castle, but we will protect it with our trusty moat." He gestured at the collection of children. "These are my knights and ladies. Care to join us?"

Emily laughed and dropped down next to him. In another minute, she was showing a little girl how to make mud squiggles out of wet sand. Together they dripped muddy designs on one of the towers. Spencer watched, obviously pleased. "I can see you've done this before," he said. "Your sand-castle days are far from over."

She looked up, the wind catching her short locks of hair. "I have experience, you know. My father and I were the best castle makers on the whole Mediterranean."

"Is that so? Well," he said proudly, "you've met your match. I come from a long line of castle makers."

Two little boys stood up, laughing and pointing. "Here comes the ocean!" they screamed gleefully, and sure enough, a huge wave rolled onto the shore, filling the moat.

"Hurry," Spencer said. "Fortify the wall."

Everyone scrambled to build up the walls of sand, but the ocean steadily proved that it was stronger than all of them. As they worked away, it slowly but surely ate away at the castle, eroding it even as they tried to save it. Spencer was working feverishly, and a huge wave came crashing around him, surrounding him with water. Mud splattered over his face, and he wiped it away, unconcerned.

"You look like the original mud man," Emily teased, which made a little girl shriek with laughter. Spencer picked her up in one sweeping motion and swung her onto his lap. They sat together in the pool of water and waited for the water to hit them again.

"A big wave!" the little girl screamed.

"Here it comes!" everyone shouted, and Emily found herself caught up in the excitement as a gush of water crashed over the castle walls. Spencer and the little girl were soaking wet and laughing as the castle slowly melted and sank.

"Who wants to sit here with us?" Spencer asked commandingly. "Who's brave enough to join me as the water attacks again?"

"Me!"

"Me, too!" the voices chorused all around him. All of the kids piled into the pool of water where Spencer was sitting, and twelve eager little faces waited for the ocean to strike again.

"Here it comes!" Spencer shouted a warning, and another wave crashed into the castle, knocking down walls and towers. Emily knelt to one side, watching Spencer with a curious blend of bemusement and admiration etched on her features. His pure joy and spontaneity were contagious; she'd never felt so alive or so free. Here was this powerful, brilliant man, surrounded by a group of happy children, and at that moment he was completely content to perch in front of a dying sand castle, letting the ocean work its inevitable force. All at once his odd philosophy made sense to her, because he was living it in front of her eyes. "Live for the moment," she whispered to herself as she stared at the happiest man she had ever seen.

By now, the castle was totally covered by the rising tide, and everyone was running into the ocean with Spencer to wash off all the mud. Only the little girl who had first joined him stayed behind, gazing worshipfully at the tall man who was diving into the ocean like a dolphin, emerging to lift the children one by one into the air.

Emily walked over to the remains of the castle and stood next to the little girl. The child looked up at her briefly with a little smile, and they both turned to watch the antics of the rest of the group in the water. Spencer saw them and waved; Emily waved back but was surprised to see the little girl also waving, as though she thought Spencer had been waving to her instead.

"I love him," said the little girl solemnly, as if it were the most natural thing in the world.

Emily's heart skipped a beat and then gave her new friend a warm smile. "I don't blame you," she said gently, looking back out to sea.

A small hand tugged at hers to get her attention, and Emily looked down into the sweetest and most sincere blue eyes she had ever seen. They looked up at her earnestly.

"Do you think he loves me?" she asked.

Emily swallowed a lump in her throat. "Of course he does," she answered. "Of course."

But there was more to it than that, and she knew it. As Spencer stood up and beckoned for them to join him, fear clutched her.

Was she falling in love with him? She shut her eyes for a second to ward off the power of the sensation.

When she opened them, the little girl was running into the water. Spencer caught her and lifted her high into the air before letting her down again in the water.

Emily was afraid that she already knew the answer to her question. It wasn't his philosophy or his advances that she had been instinctively fighting all week. It was something far more profound.

But that wasn't what frightened her. As she watched him diving under a wave, she had to ask herself if a man like him could ever fall in love with someone like her. A shadow of doubt crossed her face, and she felt her heart sink. She was so boxed in, so correct, so . . . rank and file.

Then, without thinking about anything at all, she bolted for the ocean and jumped in, letting a wave engulf her until she was in his arms, feeling like a woman who had suddenly gotten more than she had bargained for.

Chapter Five

Emily gazed up at the façade of the elegant hotel. "The Waldorf Astoria," she said. "So this is where you live."

"When I'm in New York." He grinned. "Which is quite often, actually. After all, Grand Central Station isn't far from here."

They got out of the cab, and Al took Emily's carrying case out of the back seat, along with Spencer's pail and shovel.

"You're going to look awfully funny walking through the lobby of the hotel like that," she remarked.

"Just as funny as yesterday," he agreed cheerfully, looking down at his briefly clad body. Emily had thrown an open shirt over her bikini, and at least it hung down to her knees. But Spencer was still wearing his bathing trunks and nothing else. "You can shower and change in my suite, and then we'll have dinner. You like pizza, don't you?"

They said good-bye to Al and walked inside the hotel, heading quickly for the elevators. Emily tried to ignore the stares, hoping to reach the safety of the elevator without mishap, but a bellhop approached them and addressed Spencer in a low, discreet voice.

"Excuse me, but uh—Mr. McIntyre—" Emily could see that he was embarrassed, and he looked around awkwardly before continuing. "Please use the service elevator next time. Or at least wear shoes in the lobby and proper attire. We don't allow bathing suits, you know." Spencer merely lifted an eyebrow, and the bellhop caught a glimpse of Emily. The bright red of her bikini was plainly visible through the light shirt, and he smiled politely. "On the other hand, miss," he said to her, "you may continue to come in just as you are."

Spencer laughed appreciatively, causing more heads to turn. Then the bellhop burst out laughing along with him, and Emily realized that she was the brunt of a joke.

"This is Charley Ross, one of the bellhops here," Spencer said. "We've known each other for years." He pointed to Emily. "Ms. Emily Moreau," he introduced her. "My new—uh—associate."

The bellhop's eyes danced. "Associate?"

"Yes. We've formed a partnership," Emily explained hastily. But the man wasn't buying it.

"Well, whatever. It's nice to know business is increasing." He turned to Spencer. "Are we on for Thursday night's poker game? I invited that sheikh from Arabia to join us. I thought it might liven things up."

"Sure, it's fine by me. As long as he can afford it. Also, see if Mr. Winchester is available next week. That old tycoon is itching to get even with me. I really cleaned him out last time." He nodded cordially as the elevator doors opened and they stepped inside.

Bellhops and Arab sheikhs and tycoons and taxi drivers. That was life with Spencer McIntyre. Emily wondered again who could tolerate such an existence. "I must say, you have a very diverse group of acquaintances," she observed carefully.

Spencer laughed. "People are all the same, really. You just need a little common denominator to bring them all together."

"Like a friendly poker game," she stated. She thought for a moment. "What are the stakes?"

"Whatever everyone can afford." He shrugged. "It's all in good fun. Why? Care to join us?"

"Sorry, I don't know how to play. Now, if you should happen to have a game of Monopoly going, that's a different story. Then you can count me in. Otherwise, forget it."

The doors opened, and they walked out. Spencer led the way to the corner suite, and she saw that the door was adorned with a sign that said "McIntyre, Inc." He worked his key in the lock and held the door open, and Emily, curious, walked inside.

She expected to see an elegant suite decorated in standard hotel-room style, but nothing prepared her for what she did see. He followed her inside as she gasped in amazement.

"Big, isn't it?" he asked congenially.

"It's a mess!"

Strewn all around the living room were papers, notebooks, files, cartons, and empty pizza boxes. Sitting on a table were dozens of unopened letters and telegrams. A small desk at the side was almost buried under the stacks of computer printout sheets, and Emily made out the familiar shape of a small personal computer next to the stack. She dropped her bag onto the sofa, on top of a pile of papers, and looked around. A few software discs lay on the bare floor; the carpet had been rolled up halfway to make room for a bunch of unopened cartons containing computer equipment. She stepped gingerly through the debris to look at the labels.

"I've got a job in Detroit next week," he said casually. "I'm taking that machine with me to set up the first computerized automobile."

"I can't believe you live like this," she said, looking at him curiously. "Doesn't a maid ever come in to clean it?"

Spencer shook his head. "I don't like anyone fooling around with my business. The maid is allowed to make the bed, change the sheets, and clean the bathroom and the kitchen, but that's it."

"Kitchen?" She peered around the cartons and saw a tiny room with an immaculate stove, refrigerator and sink. A lone can of Spaghetti-os sat on the counter. "Well, that's a switch," she said tartly. "At least you're not a total slob."

She swallowed that last word, but he was heading into the bathroom, not even listening to her. "I'll just take a quick shower, and then you can take one. Is pizza all right? Goldberg's pizza is the best in New York."

He disappeared into the bathroom and closed the door. Emily ventured over to the table with all of the unopened mail. All of the correspondence was addressed to McIntyre, Inc. at the infamous post-office box at Grand Central Station. The letters came from all over the world, and some of the postmarks were over a month old. She picked one up and examined it. It was from a large company in New York. Underneath the letter was a telegram from the same company. On an impulse, she opened the letter and scanned the contents. It was a job offer, and her eyes opened wide as she read the terms. They were offering thirty thousand dollars to fix a system. "I can't believe this," she muttered. "And he didn't even open it." She ripped open the telegram and shook her head in disbelief. It was a second offer for the same job, but this time it was a plea, and the money had gone up by fifteen percent.

Growing more and more excited, she randomly chose another letter and then another and another. She skimmed through them, astonished by the discovery she had just made.

"Do you always open other people's mail?" Spencer

asked, standing over her. She looked up, saw that he was dripping wet and clad only in a towel that was knotted around his waist, and quickly looked down. "You've got job offers here by the dozen!"

He only shrugged.

"Hey, partner," she said boldly. "You've been holding out on me."

"I can only handle one job at a time," he said briefly. "I pick and choose the ones that interest me most." He lifted a few of the envelopes in the air and tossed them nonchalantly onto the floor as if they were scrap paper. One caught his eye, and he fished it out of the pile and tossed it onto the sofa. It landed on some books and slid onto the floor. "I might take that one," he said. Emily was flabbergasted. "Now go and take a shower," he commanded. "I'm starving. Maybe we'll go to a movie after. There's a new Spielberg flick that I want to see."

Emily was still gazing at him in astonishment. She tore her eyes away from him and looked slowly around the room. "What other surprises do you have hidden under all this mess?" She walked over to the sofa and picked up the letter he had just tossed. "Get dressed and give me some time," she ordered. "Go out and get a pizza and bring it back here." She looked up and faced him squarely, still avoiding the towel. "It will take me hours to go through all of this."

"What are you talking about?" he said peevishly. "I thought we were going out!"

"Go get the pizza," she said, waving him off. "I've got work to do." She jerked her thumb toward the door. "Now get dressed and scram. That's an order." She smiled sweetly. "We're partners now, remember?"

"Esmerelda isn't going to like this," he said, backing away. "She said you weren't supposed to work until—"

"Out!" she shouted. "That is an order!"

She became completely involved in her work and barely noticed as he disappeared into the bedroom and came out a few minutes later, dressed in his usual uniform of jeans and an open shirt.

He left and was back in less than half an hour, and in that time she had begun to compile a list of all the job offers he had received. Spencer put the pizza down and took out a slice, eating it hungrily as he watched her.

"Having fun?" he asked. Emily said nothing. "How long have you been suffering from this malady?" he continued as she threw a bunch of envelopes into the garbage. "Are all those the jobs you're rejecting?" He munched the pizza and kept watching her as she went on sorting the mail. After another slice, he became impatient. He fished out a slice for her and held it under her nose. She ignored it, pushing it away as if it were an annoying fly, and continued filing papers into the garbage. Finally, she looked up and gave him a radiant smile.

"I've got some interesting news," she said, still refusing the slice of pizza. She got up and stretched. "I made some calls while you were out to some of my old pals at Fenton who lost their jobs." She waved a piece of paper with names and phone numbers on it in front of his face. "Would you believe that out of fourteen unemployed programmers—"

"All of them have found jobs," Spencer interrupted. "And for more money, right?"

Emily was stunned. "How did you know?"

"My dear, naive Ms. Moreau," he said, coming over and flipping through her neatly processed stacks. "All of these offers for consulting work are very well and fine, but I don't have time for all of them, and there's a brain drain on the market."

"What's a brain drain?"

"There are simply not enough computer programmers to go around." He looked through the pile and threw the envelopes into the garbage one by one. "It's a classic case of supply and demand. We are fortunate to be in a seller's market. And we, the programmers, are the sellers. There aren't enough of us, and they need us. Badly."

"Which drives the price for our services higher."

He patted her on the head with mock condescension. "By George, I think she's got it."

"Then we'll just have to pay our programmers more than any other consulting firm. By the looks of some of these jobs, that won't be too hard to do." She held up an accounting sheet and handed it to him. "This is a list of the total amount of work being offered, minus costs. You're looking at pure profit."

He didn't even bother to look at it. "And just whom do you plan on hiring for all these jobs?" he asked coldly.

Emily stood up and retrieved the envelopes that he had just thrown away. "If you had waited for me to finish," she said, "I called twelve people, and four of them were willing to come work for us." She smiled up at him triumphantly and handed the pile back to him. He thumbed through it again with a slight frown. Then he threw them abruptly back into the garbage.

"No," he said flatly. "I'm a loner. I work alone."

"You mean you *were* working alone. What about me, your new associate?"

He looked down at the floor and then back up at her. His mouth turned into a tight little line, and his eyes flashed decidedly. "Just forget about that."

"What?" She was shocked. "Then what is all this about?"

"I can't have a partner," he said. "I told you, I'm a loner. You wanted to call yourself my associate at

Fenton's party, so I let you, but don't get the wrong idea."

"Why, you manipulator!" she shot back. "When you get desperate, you say whatever pops into your head to get me to do what you want. Then when the trouble is resolved, you crawl back into your crumby hotel room and—and—" She held up the remains of the pizza, which had grown soggy and cold. "And cold pizza," she finished. "Is that what you want out of life?"

"What I want out of life is not your concern," he shouted. "I built this business up out of nothing. Who are you to come in here like the queen of Sheba and start criticizing it? You don't know anything about it! These job offers are mine!" he said, grabbing the pile of envelopes and clutching it in his fist. "Mine, not yours. They want me, not you."

She didn't flinch. "They want McIntyre, Inc." She stood up and faced him. "So what's it going to be, Spencer? Are we in business or not? Because if we're not, I'm walking out that door."

He marched over to the door and opened it with a flourish. "So long," he said pointedly, with a sweeping gesture.

There was nothing to do but walk out with all the dignity she could muster. She was hurt and angry and confused. She thought he had been chasing her all week, and all he had wanted was her help in getting through a difficult job. And she had fallen for his line like a naive schoolgirl. She swallowed hard and headed for the door, avoiding his fiery stare. The worst part of it was that he was probably right. Who was she to think that she could walk in and take over his business? Something like that had to be earned, just as he had earned it. She was still good old rank and file Emily. Just another good soldier taking orders. All her life she had been afraid to make waves, to do something different, to be an innovator . . .

But even as her thoughts tumbled through her head, her father's stern words came back to her. "Fight back, Emily. Don't take things lying down." She came up to Spencer and suppressed the shiver that went through her as she grazed against his body. As she passed through the door, a wave of resistance shot through her. Maybe he didn't feel about her the way she was beginning to feel about him, but she still had to live with herself. He had called her his associate, and that was a fact. Fight back, Emily, she said to herself. That's an order.

"Yes, sir!" she said aloud, turning on her heel and throwing the door back open just as Spencer was closing it.

"Ow!" he cried. "Oh, my God!"

She peered hesitantly around the door, but he wasn't there. Then her gaze traveled down, and to her horror, she saw Spencer sprawled out on the floor, his hand over his right eye. He slowly lowered his hand, and she saw that his right eye now matched the left one.

"I don't believe this," he moaned, gingerly feeling the injured area.

"Don't move," she said, running to the refrigerator. She found some ice cubes and wrapped them hastily in a towel. "Here, try this," she said, running back to him. He sat up slowly and applied the ice pack to his eye. "A matching pair, Mr. McIntyre," she said briskly. "Very good. And don't tell me you don't deserve it. You do."

"I know," he said lamely.

"No wonder you're a loner," she said. "You can't even get along with me. I came up with a good idea. I was even willing to work on it by myself, and all you did was throw me out."

"I told you, I'm not good with people." He lowered the ice pack to reveal his swollen eye. Emily gently pushed it back, holding her hand over his. "I'm a corporation of one," he added.

"Two."

Spencer sighed. "Emily, think. Why do you think I went to the beach alone?"

"Because of the heat wave."

"Because I didn't want to cramp your style, and I didn't want you to cramp mine." He got up and went over to the couch. "When it comes to business, I work best alone."

Emily listened, but she didn't believe it. She could see that he believed what he was saying, but something didn't ring true. The image of Spencer on the beach, taking charge of a group of children, came back to her. She thought about Al and the bellhop and all of the relationships that Spencer had maintained for years. He organized poker games with odd assortments of people, and yet he didn't think he was good with people. She looked at him. "I want you to trust me, Spencer."

He didn't say anything, eyeing her suspiciously.

"Now I'm going to go over all these job offers again, and you're not going to stop me." Still he said nothing, and that gave her courage to continue. "It doesn't make sense to turn away business. You got me into this, and I'm not leaving. I intend to stay, and as your partner. Unless, of course, your word means nothing."

"My word?"

"Yes. We have a verbal agreement to form a partnership. It was the only way you could get me to work on the Fenton project, and I accepted."

"Me and my big mouth," he mumbled.

"Yes. You and your big mouth have earned you two black eyes and a business partner. From now on, I'll do

the talking, and you do some listening for a change."
She expected him to blow up at her at any moment;
instead, his mouth curved up into a tiny smile.

"What is so amusing?" she asked.

He got up and came over to her, looking down into
her eyes. "Esmerelda was right about you. You do have
amazing hidden potential."

She smiled. "So do we have a deal?"

He smiled back. "All right, Emily Moreau. We're
partners. But the name of the firm remains McIntyre,
Inc." He held out his hand.

Emily took it, expecting a firm handshake, but he
pulled her close and took her in his arms. "Now wait a
minute," she protested. "This isn't part of the deal."

"What's the matter?" he asked, still holding her
close. "You can't have it both ways, Emily. You can't
expect to be my partner and not expect me to want to
make love to you. Because I do. And I don't take no for
an answer."

She was a little flustered at such a direct statement,
and before she had time to react, his mouth was
claiming hers. His arms were strong and insistent as he
crushed her against his body, and she yielded, letting
the waves of pleasure wash over her. This kiss was long,
his tongue invading her mouth and exploring its interior
with hunger. She clung to him, unable to resist. The
sparks of desire that had been building between them
all day were fanned into leaping flames. She was
helpless under the tender assault, her senses whirling as
she savored the sweetness of his touch. Her heart
began to pound as his hands roamed over her curves,
drinking in her femininity with raw male pleasure. He
left small, fiery kisses across her face and down her
neck, making her arch her head back to ease his way.

His hands found her shoulders and wandered restlessly to the top button of her shirt. She was still wearing the shirt over her bikini, and she gasped when he deftly undid the front and pushed the sides apart. Now her body was open to him, and she wasn't sure if she wanted to stop him or beg him to continue. Why would she ever want to stop this sweet fire that threatened to overwhelm her with delight? Her shirt slid from her shoulders and fell to the floor; she felt deliciously bare and wanton in front of him. His gray eyes were filled with hunger and told her that she was every inch a desirable woman. His breathing was ragged as he drew her close again, molding his hands around the supple length of her back. Her breasts swelled over the top of the red bikini, provocatively within his grasp. He cupped them willingly, groaning with passion as he lowered his head to kiss the soft curves. Emily trembled as his hands reached for the narrow straps that held the bikini top in place, and her hands followed his instinctively to stop him.

"No," she breathed through her own desire. "Please."

"For God's sake, Emily," he said hoarsely. "This was meant to be. You can't fight it any more than I can."

"But—" Whatever she was about to say was interrupted rudely by the ringing of the telephone. She looked toward the jangling instrument automatically, but he turned her head back to face him.

"Ignore it," he commanded, his hands sliding down her arms.

"I—I can't," she protested weakly. "I made some important calls before, and—" She broke away and dashed over to the phone. Her heart was still racing, but she forced her voice to sound calm and business-like.

"Hello? Yes, it is . . . Oh, Mr. Winchester! I'm so glad you called." She looked up at Spencer sharply, and he returned her glance with a dark frown. "Yes, that's right. I'm glad you got my message . . . You are? That's wonderful! Of course, we'd be glad to . . . What? Oh, uh, very recently. Yes, it's a very recent development . . . Yes, we've got four people available immediately . . . You will?" Her eyes brightened. "That's excellent, Mr. Winchester. Very good. All right, I'll talk to you tomorrow." She hung up the phone and gave Spencer a bright-eyed glance. "Uh— that was Mr. Winchester," she said.

"So I gather." There was a pause. "Well, what did he want, Emily?"

She couldn't bite back a huge smile. "I just got us our first outside account. Winchester is hiring our four employees to program his computers in Japan." She stopped, waiting for a reaction, but there was none. "He's paying all their expenses," she added hopefully. Still there was no response. "We'll clear a thirty percent profit off the top," she finished, and this time it was Spencer who couldn't hide a smile. She laughed triumphantly. "You don't object to making money, do you?"

"No." He shook his head. "I can't say I do."

"Good." She picked up her shirt and slipped it back on, quickly buttoning it. Spencer didn't look as if he liked that development, but Emily sat down at the desk and looked up at him in a thoroughly businesslike way. "Now, where can I find the phone number of his company in Japan? I didn't ask him."

"Top drawer."

She opened the drawer and was disconcerted to find dozens of pieces of torn paper floating around at random. But she wasn't surprised. Nothing about that room surprised her anymore. Patiently, she waded through all of the scraps until she found what she was looking for. The number was scribbled on the back of a matchbook.

Spencer strolled over curiously and watched as she turned to the personal computer. "What's the code for getting into this thing?" she asked.

"Just turn it on. Any questions you have, Bruce will supply."

"Bruce?" She smiled.

He spread his hands in a gesture of explanation. "Ever since Esmerelda appeared, it seemed like the thing to do. This computer is definitely a he."

He spoke so seriously that she swallowed a laugh. Esmerelda was obviously catching. She began to work expertly with the computer, but after a minute, she looked up in exasperation.

"What's the matter?" Spencer had become suddenly laconic. He was watching Emily change in front of his eyes, and the transition was rather awesome.

"Your file system. Names and addresses of all your clients. A billing system." She waited, saw he wasn't going to answer and practically exploded. "Where are they? I can't find them."

Spencer pointed to his head. "All in here," he said proudly. "All in here."

Emily shook her head, completely perplexed. Then she took out all of the little scraps of paper from the drawers and began sorting them alongside the computer. "First thing tomorrow, we hire ourselves a secretary."

"No!" He surprised her with his vehemence. "One addition is enough. You know, Emily, I think I've created a monster."

Emily didn't care. She began to efficiently sort,

process and code into the computer as she began her new venture. Spencer was hovering over her, and after a while, she looked up with a determined glint in her eye.

"I won't be needing you for a while," she said coolly. "Enjoy yourself. Go see a movie. I'll see you later."

She went back to her work without another word, and Spencer stood there watching her for a few more minutes. Then, realizing that it would be futile to argue, he ruefully rubbed his two swollen eyes and ambled grumpily out the door, mumbling something about the dangers of letting a woman in your life.

The moment he was gone, Emily stopped, looked up from her work and grinned. She wondered for one capricious moment if Fenton wasn't singing the very same tune. Then, with the smile still on her face, she went back to the business at hand.

"I don't believe it," Spencer kept repeating when he returned three hours later. He walked slowly around the living room of the suite while Emily remained seated at the computer, her arms folded in smug satisfaction.

The place was immaculate. The clutter and chaos had been replaced by organized neatness. Two large bins were filled with all the paper and debris that had been thrown out, and the surface of the desk was clean. She held a single envelope in her hand, and he picked it up curiously. It was addressed to Mr. Winchester.

"Our first new client," she said. "It's a bill for the first half of the payment in advance."

"Why?"

"I thought we'd need money to work with," she answered, surprised.

"I have money to work with."

"Not your money," she pointed out. "Our money."

"I see." He sat down on the now-empty sofa and looked at her. "And which one of us, may I ask, is going to Japan?"

"Neither one of us." She smiled and turned to the computer, keying in a fast question. He walked over and saw a list of names there, complete with addresses and phone numbers. "Our new staff," she explained. "They're all on their way to Japan, courtesy of Winchester."

He took a deep breath and let it out slowly.

"What's the matter?" Emily asked impatiently. "Now we're really in business." He remained silent, and she began to grow nervous. "Look, if it's the control you want, you can have it. You can decide on all the jobs, and of course you'll get first choice. It's just that now we'll make more money and have a bigger hold on the consulting market." He walked away, and she followed him anxiously with her eyes, wondering what on earth he was thinking. "Spencer . . . ?"

He turned and looked at her, then looked away again. He began to circle the room, picking up things and putting them down, as if he still couldn't believe his eyes. Every so often he looked back at her again, shaking his head, and she waited with a quizzical expression. He wandered into the bedroom and came out again, finally sitting down on the sofa.

"You've metamorphosed," he said.

She smiled proudly. "No more rank and file, right?" She indicated a notebook. "These are the most promising job offers. I'll call them all tomorrow, and I'll ask Esmerelda for a list of the programmers who were fired on Monday." He nodded, still stunned. "So," she said, sitting back with a satisfied grin, "how was the movie?"

"What? Oh, the movie. I didn't go. I walked around

for a while, but my eye started hurting again, so I stopped in a bar I know and had a few drinks. I did some thinking."

"About what?"

He crooked a finger for her to join him on the sofa, and after a moment's hesitation, she did. He looked so bewildered sitting there by himself. He took her hand firmly in his.

"Uh—would you like to know about the filing and billing systems I set up for us?" she asked nervously.

"No. I don't. Come here." He pulled her close, but she resisted him. "What's the matter, Emily? You can't fight me forever. I've decided I'm going to make love to you, and that's final. You can fix up my business to your heart's content, and I must say, you seem to be very good at it. But I've watched you blossom into a woman before my eyes, and the result is very, very intriguing." He tried to embrace her again, but he saw the shadow that crossed her face and stopped impatiently. "What is it now, Emily?"

"It's—it's just that I don't think it should be like this." She spoke in a tremulous whisper, and he frowned.

"What do you mean, like this? Like what?"

She could barely explain herself in such a precarious position, but her thoughts were tumbling through her head. She wanted him—she had no doubt about that. And he obviously wanted her. But she knew that there was more, much more, to her feelings, and she had a distinct sense of doubt that he could possibly be feeling the same way about her. So far he seemed to regard her as a curiosity, an amusement. He was so free, so devoid of commitment, that she knew in her heart she could never hope to pin him down beyond a stolen night in his arms. There had to be more to it than that. And there just wasn't.

"I—I think I'd better be going home now" was all she said.

"Home! What do you mean? I thought—"

"I can see what you thought." It came out more cuttingly than she had intended, and she stopped, taking a deep breath. "It's too soon, Spencer," she added, stalling for time. She looked up at him beseechingly, knowing he was unconvinced. She tried to look as innocently earnest as she felt, but he looked so funny all of a sudden, sitting there scowling with his two black eyes, that she burst out laughing.

"I'm glad you find this amusing," he said stonily, drawing back coldly and standing up.

"I'm sorry, Spencer," she said, choking back her laughter. "It's just that . . . you look so funny!" A fresh peal of laughter escaped her, and he gave her a murderous look.

"Don't toy with me, Emily," he said in such a commanding voice that her laughter was cut short. "I'm not a patient man. I have no time for foolish games." He walked over to the door and opened it. "If you want to leave, go ahead." His face softened. "I'll see you tomorrow. But be prepared."

She got up and walked toward the door, deciding to take him at his word. She would hail a cab from the lobby and escape the stares of people on the street.

"Good night, Emily," he said softly. She stopped and looked at him.

"Good night, Spencer," she said. He bent down and kissed her gently. She didn't move. He took her fully in his arms and kissed her again, this time using all of his power and skill to make her melt against him. Emily's heart soared at his fiery, persuasive touch. She could feel her breasts straining against the bikini top as he slowly massaged her back and invaded her mouth with his tongue. All of her former resolve fled. What did the next day matter when she had such an unbearably lovely sensation to savor then? Maybe she'd been wrong about him. Maybe he had more feelings than she had thought. She hadn't really given him a chance. The kiss was followed by another and then another. She was completely lost in the swirling of colors before her closed eyelids, willingly letting the fire course through her blood.

Spencer drew his mouth from hers. Her head fell back, silently ordering him to continue to make love to her, but nothing happened. Slowly, her eyes fluttered open, and she looked at him, puzzled.

"Good night, Emily," he said softly. "I told you. I have no desire to make love to a high and mighty virgin. Or even one with stars in her eyes." He smiled slowly. "When I make love to you, there will be nothing to stand between us. I want you to be very, very sure."

She had been sure, but suddenly she wasn't any longer. A slight frown creased her forehead, and his smile became knowing. "You see, Emily?" he said mirroring her own thoughts. "You aren't so sure, are you?" He kissed her forehead. "I'll see you tomorrow." He ushered her out without giving her time to answer, and in a moment she was standing out in the hall, not sure what had just happened but glad that she would have time to think about it. Spencer was the most confusing man she had ever met.

Chapter Six

"So to summarize for the board exactly what we've been able to accomplish with Esmerelda during the past week, I will refer to this chart." Emily stood in front of the twelve men on Fenton's executive board several days later, wearing a brand-new black suit that was considerably more stylish and well fitted than anything she had worn before. It was complemented by a simple but stunning white silk blouse and the high-heeled black shoes she had worn to Fenton's party. Fenton himself was there, puffing furiously on a cigarette as he listened to the presentation being given by his two consultants. Spencer sat quietly off to one side next to a large easel holding charts and graphs. His two shiners were still somewhat evident, but they'd faded to a great extent, so he now simply looked interestingly debauched and no longer looked like the victim of a brawl.

Emily pointed to the chart resting on the easel, and everyone turned to look at it expectantly. She thought their presentation was going well, but it was hard to tell. When she'd described the ways in which they had cleverly gotten Esmerelda to relinquish some of her power, Fenton had seemed pleased. But most of the time, the gruff magnate maintained a neutral expression, as did Spencer. She was beginning to feel wedged between two powerful men, but the rest of the board members were clearly pleased at her report. Thompson gave her an approving smile from time to time, especially when she described how they had taught Esmerelda to negotiate.

"So if I am to understand you, Ms. Moreau," Fenton finally broke in, "you are saying that we are really stuck with this Esmerelda business for good."

"That's just the point," she said carefully. "The current condition of Esmerelda is quite flexible. We're dealing with a highly sophisticated electronic brain that luckily believes in fair play."

"Fair play!" Fenton repeated.

"That's right. Right now I'm concentrating on getting Esmerelda to give up more and more of her power through negotiation. For example, she can no longer call a coffee break for an entire factory."

A ripple of approval went through the room, encouraging her to continue.

"But," she added, holding up one finger, "she will try to find other ways to ease production if she feels it is necessary. After all, she does have in her memory banks a working knowledge of industrial psychological axioms and theories pertaining to the human element in manufacturing."

This was met by total silence, and Spencer quickly hid a smile behind one hand. "Meaning?" Fenton asked abruptly.

"Meaning—well—uh . . ." She stopped, searching for the right words, and Spencer helped her out.

"Meaning," he interjected smoothly, "that the computer controls all of your paper work. It will still do everything you want it to do. But if you go against the guidelines by which you hired your employees—if you make them work beyond their individual capacities or fire too many people without a logical reason, the computer will cut you off without even an explanation."

The group reacted with gasps and deep frowns of disapproval. "I'd rather have that damn computer destroyed first!" Fenton shouted.

"Esmerelda already knows that," Emily said as gently as she could. "She has already guessed that you will pull the plug on her, and she's ready to compromise with you. But before you do anything, I'd like you to look at the chart we've prepared so that you'll know exactly how to behave with her. Otherwise, she'll shut down all by herself."

Spencer turned the easel to a different angle so that they could all see it better, but again he let Emily control the report.

"The rules, gentlemen," Emily began. She pointed to the first page of the chart. "We begin with etiquette." She looked around as if expecting some objection, but there was none, so she continued. "I don't believe there is anything new to say on this subject except that Esmerelda has informed me that a few of you have been talking back to her using four-letter words. The Paris office is especially guilty of this. She retaliated by changing an order for fifty cases of champagne that were supposed to be delivered from Épernay."

"What did she change it to?" Fenton asked, as if against his better judgment.

"Fifty cases of Wild Irish Rose." Laughter erupted, and she took advantage of this to add, "Remember, she is capable of retaliatory logic based on sociological data as well as economic and anthropological records."

"Would you mind translating that, Ms. Moreau?" Fenton was growing impatient, and she hurried to explain.

"It means that Esmerelda can counter any shenanigans with the appropriate punishment. Most computers will simply refuse to act on a command they haven't been programmed for, but Esmerelda is able to handle anything that comes her way." She turned the chart to the next page, and Spencer obligingly folded the old one behind the easel. "Now we come to the poetry. I'm afraid it can't be removed. It will be there forever." The look on Fenton's face prompted her to add hastily, "However, we have gotten her to underline the words that comprise the actual answer to the question that was asked. She will spew out information at top speed, and it will still be in verse. But now the information that you requested will be underlined. So if you don't like the poetry, just go to the pertinent data by looking at the underlined words."

Fenton sat silently absorbing this.

"Third," Emily continued. "When it comes to sending flowers to employees and—uh—arranging plane tickets for our executives—"

"Plane tickets!" Fenton stated murderously.

"Uh—Mr. Fenton?" It was Thompson.

"Well, what is it?"

"Well, sir, you see, the computer is hooked up to international travel services. We simply state our destinations, and the reservations are made. Esmerelda has been rescheduling and reworking destinations to comply with vacation time. Last week I had to go to our Buffalo office, but Esmerelda knows I have family in Albany. So she got me a flight that stops there, and I realized too late that it was my destination for the night." He turned to Emily. "How did she know to do that, anyway?"

"That is the crux of the issue," Emily replied. "The computer has been reprogrammed to cross-reference all information in its data banks. It's practically a free thinker, and as we have all seen, a real lady."

Fenton wasn't interested. "And what about the culprit who did all this?" he asked. "Did you find out anything more about who she could be?"

"She?" Spencer asked, as if Fenton knew something that he didn't.

"Whatever," Fenton answered with an impatient gesture. "I just said that because the damn computer turned into a she."

But Spencer's face had changed suddenly, as something very logical and very, very interesting dawned on him. "Well, I'll be," he mumbled to himself. Emily watched him. She'd spent almost all of her time either at the Fenton offices or with Spencer in his hotel room, and both of them had remained coolly, almost elaborately professional. Neither of them had ever made a reference to the night they had officially started their partnership, and they were, for all the world, simply two business people solving a corporate problem. Now, as Emily looked at him, she assumed that he was thinking about the problem at hand. But suddenly he chuckled as if at some private joke, and then, as if something had finally occurred to him, he shook his head. He looked around the room, and his bemused expression became serious.

"Whoever she is, gentlemen," he said quietly, "she was clever enough to fool even me."

At his words, Emily froze. She looked at him fearfully, and he met her gaze with a triumphant, knowing one of his own. She knew in that moment that he knew, and she wondered frantically what he would do. His gray eyes held hers for a long moment, making sure she was squirming, and then he got up nonchalantly and went over to the terminal at the back of the room.

Emily's hands were shaking, and she clutched them together so that no one would notice. "Uh—Mr. Fenton," she said, trying to regain control. Fenton looked from Spencer to Emily, one eyebrow lifted quizzically. "If you'd like to try it now, Esmerelda would like to talk with you again."

"Again?" Fenton scowled. "The last time that computer talked to me, she assured me that I'd never get any information out of her again unless I 'shaped up.'" He looked around the room accusingly. "Shaped up! Can you imagine that?"

"And that's when you threatened to disconnect her?" Emily prodded gently.

"Then it was a threat. Now it's a promise." Fenton stood up and addressed his vice-presidents. "There's one more thing I want to know," he said. "How has business been since this thing started? Is it up or down?"

"Well, actually, sir," Thompson said, brightening, "it's been up by three percent."

There was a short, potent silence. No one moved except for Spencer, who was ignoring all of them, busily working with the computer at the back of the room.

"Even with the coffee breaks?" Fenton asked suspiciously. "Even with extra vacation days?" Thompson nodded. "Well, it had better be. This company was created without a computer. My grandfather built it out of nothing. If production goes down, I'll pull the plug on that electronic monster and go back to the way things were. I don't mind the flowers, and I don't even mind a few side trips by my executives. But I won't stand for this!" He strode over to Emily's charts detailing the etiquette procedure and the rhyme schemes and ripped it into shreds. "I won't play games with that thing. This is a business, not a poetry-reading group in Greenwich Village. I want my information straight, without all these ridiculous fringe benefits. And if you can't get me that, then I want nothing except the head of the irresponsible maniac who destroyed it!"

Emily blanched. She was beginning to feel nauseous, but Thompson unwittingly jumped in and saved her.

"But sir," he said, "production *has* been up. Isn't that the most important thing?"

"Yes," Fenton said firmly. "And maybe it proves that we don't need this contraption anymore, anyway."

Spencer had stopped fiddling with the computer, and he turned around and looked at Fenton seriously. "The cost of transferring all the information onto a new computer would be astronomical," he said. "Besides, what makes you think the computer isn't directly responsible for the profit increase?"

"But how could that be possible?" Fenton demanded. "With all of those coffee breaks and all the time wasted trying to get the computer to give a straight answer."

Spencer shrugged. "Ask her."

Fenton looked at Emily, who paled again. "Who, her?"

"No." Spencer smiled. "Esmerelda." He beckoned to Fenton, who got up and came over to the terminal. Spencer let him sit in the chair, and Emily came up behind him to watch.

"All right," Fenton said with a note of challenge in his voice. "I want to know the precise amount of time our piece goods factory in Pennsylvania has been in operation for the last thirty days." He glared at Spencer.

"Don't look at me," Spencer said. He gestured to the computer, and Emily discreetly helped him to key in his code. Then he typed in the question with two fingers while the executives all gathered around curiously to watch.

As they waited, Spencer caught Emily's eye and smiled. "I've got to admit," he said, looking straight at her, "it's a brilliant program. Absolutely brilliant."

GOOD MORNING, MR. FENTON, Esmerelda greeted the president. I HOPE WE CAN COME TO TERMS ON THAT MATTER OF ETIQUETTE.

"Apologize to her," Spencer said.

Fenton opened his mouth to protest, but Emily quickly reached around him and typed for him. I AM SO SORRY ABOUT YESTERDAY. PLEASE FURNISH THE FOLLOWING INFORMATION.

Fenton looked up at Emily, and with a resigned sigh, he typed in his question. Spencer was looking at Emily during all of this, and she tried desperately to avoid his gaze. But it was impossible as he riveted her eyes with his. He was mocking her, sizing her up, and she knew it. All week long he'd been giving her these unexpected, curious looks, as if he'd been analyzing her and trying to figure her out. Now his opinion of her was clear. He knew that she had created Esmerelda—that she *was,* in effect, Esmerelda. And it didn't seem to bother him at all. If anything, he seemed to find the whole thing fascinating and amusing at the same time.

"Here it is," Fenton said, and everyone leaned forward to read the computer's response.

```
HICKORY DICKORY DOCK,
THE FACTORY RAN ROUND THE CLOCK.
EXCEPT FOR TWO BREAKS
FOR EMPLOYEES' FAIR SHAKES,
THERE WAS THREE PERCENT INCREASE IN
STOCK.
```

"Ah, Mother Goose again," Spencer said with congenial interest, still looking straight at Emily. "Most interesting. Now that I think about it, there's an underlying sophistication to it that I just can't get over." He smiled disarmingly. "Brilliant," he continued. "A simple insertion of a new language into an existing system. But this one is melted in so that it can never be removed."

Fenton looked up angrily. "How the hell can it be inserted without my knowledge? I'm the only one with the code to enable a new program to go into the computer!"

"Unless someone figured out a way to get around it." Spencer had not taken his eyes from Emily's face. "Brilliant," he repeated. "Beautiful and brilliant."

Emily wanted to crawl under a rock. Spencer was driving closer and closer to home, and Fenton was only getting angrier.

"I'd like to get my hands around the culprit's throat," the president growled.

"I'd like to get my arms around her," Spencer said so quietly that only Emily heard him.

"So production was up. It's true," Thompson offered.

"No thanks to Esmerelda!" Fenton snapped.

"Don't be so hasty," Spencer said calmly, finally turning away from Emily. "I've seen this sort of thing before on a less complex level." Fenton raised an eyebrow. "Esmerelda is programmed to deal on a human level. To her, people are mathematical equations. Happiness and sadness can be assigned numerical values." He smiled sardonically and turned right back to Emily, pinning her with his laser stare. "Our culprit simply gave Esmerelda the ability to translate those equations into emotional commands instead of statistics and graphs. She is obviously a deeply sensitive person —and a very creative, whimsical one, even though she doesn't know it. But she can't keep hiding. I'm bound to find her, and she knows it."

Emily couldn't stand it. She searched wildly for

something to say, something that would distract his attention. "The information is all there, Mr. Fenton," she stammered. "It hasn't really changed so much."

"I told you, I don't care!" Fenton exploded. "If you can't get rid of Esmerelda, then I want the whole system dismantled."

Spencer dropped his casual demeanor and leaned one elbow on the side of the terminal. Everyone looked at him with respect, Emily included. "Let's put all our cards on the table, Fenton," he said. "You can't afford to do that, and you know it. The cost to reprogram would be in the millions, and you would lose an incalculable amount of data." He banged his fist on the terminal. "You're stuck with this sweetheart of a computer, and that's the truth. All we can do is to continue to negotiate with her. But frankly, I don't have the time or the personnel to do it."

Fenton's face dropped, and his eyes flashed angrily. "I hired you for a job, McIntyre. You're saying you didn't succeed, so—"

"So you owe me nothing. There's a first time for everything, me included." Without another word, Spencer whipped out a checkbook and began writing. "Here's a check for your deposit of fifty thousand dollars." He ripped out the check and handed it to Fenton.

"So the great Spencer McIntyre quits!" Fenton got up and headed for the door. "I should have known better than to hire you. By tomorrow morning, your name will be mud all over New York."

Emily jumped between them, barely aware of what she was saying. "Wait a minute, Mr. Fenton. Just because my partner has given up doesn't mean our company has to quit." Fenton lifted an eyebrow, and Spencer looked at her in surprise.

"But, Emily—" he began.

"Let me handle this, Spencer," she insisted. He sat back and watched her curiously. "Spencer gave Esmerelda the ability to negotiate," she said to Fenton, "and I will continue the negotiations. I may not be able to get rid of Esmerelda. And I can't tell you how she got into the computer in the first place. But I can tame her. Put her on a leash, so to speak." She tried a smile. "We've gotten to be good friends over the past week."

Fenton looked from Emily to Spencer, as if amused that a woman was handling McIntyre. He handed the check back to Spencer without a word, but Emily snatched it from him and gave it back.

"This job is free," she said. "Absolutely."

Fenton shrugged. "As you wish." He opened the door. "Find me the person who started this disaster in the first place, and I'll write you another check." He left the room, followed by his entourage.

"Well," Spencer said cheerfully when they had gone. "I just may get that check back. Followed by a lawsuit that will probably destroy me."

"What do you mean?" Emily frowned. Now that the meeting was over, she thought she could relax. But with Spencer, relaxation was often an elusive goal.

"Congratulations, partner," he said. "You just set me up for the kill." He kicked at a chair, shaking the table violently. A glass ashtray toppled from the table, falling neatly into the trash can. They both looked at it for a second, and then they looked at each other. Emily's eyes were fearful. "Do you realize what you've done?" he demanded. He spun around, his hands on his head. "What an idiot I was! What a blind idiot! Asking Esmerelda to supply me with the best person to fix her. And who should she recommend but the very person who programmed her in the first place. And I fell right into the trap!"

"What trap?" Emily was close to tears. "There was

no trap. I was on vacation. Ask Fenton; ask Esmerelda! You saw me on my last day. I was fired. Finished. I went off to Maine to visit my father, and it was then that Esmerelda was put into the computer. I threw that damn tape into the garbage, Spencer! Someone must have fished it out and—"

"And just happens to know the security code to get into the brains of that machine?" He looked skeptical.

"Don't you believe me?" Emily was stung, and she fought back her tears.

He sighed. "I do believe you, Emily. But that's not answering any questions. Fenton's code is too hard to break." He shut his eyes for a moment, thinking hard.

"But what does it matter now?" she asked. He seemed to be taking it awfully hard. "And why is that your problem?"

His eyes flew open, and he came up to her and grabbed her shoulders, squeezing hard. "Think, Emily." His grip was like iron, and she winced, but he didn't let up. "I knew you were the last employee to go. Then Fenton discovers this huge problem, for which I charge him a fat fee to fix. Suddenly, after years of working alone, I hire you. And then it is discovered that you were the culprit."

Emily cupped her hands over her mouth as she realized what he was saying. "Oh, my God," she gasped. "Oh, no. They'll think you conspired with me to ruin the computer just to walk away with a job!"

He nodded grimly. "It's like being a newspaper reporter and blowing up a bridge just so you can write an exclusive story about it."

Emily looked at him bravely. "We'll just have to tell him the truth."

"Forget it." He spoke vehemently, and she knew that he meant it. "Don't be naive, Emily. It's out of the question."

"But we have to tell him. It's unethical not to."

His face softened. "Maybe. But we'll tell him after all the statistics are in. If profit goes up, it'll be easier to break the news."

"But what if profits go down?" It was a horrible question, but she had to ask it.

"Then we'll go down together." He forced a smile. "Right—partner?"

Emily said nothing, knowing that he must hate her. He had to. She had unwittingly trapped him into a perilous situation that could destroy everything he'd built up for himself. She looked down at the floor to hide the fresh tears that were budding in her eyes. How could she have been so foolish? She wished fervently for a hole to open up in the floor so that she could sink into it and disappear.

In spite of herself, she looked up curiously. His face was gentle, and he crooked one finger under her chin. "We don't have time for guilt and recrimination," he said. "Now why don't you just tell me everything— from the beginning."

She sighed and sat down at the conference table, relating the whole crazy incident, from that fateful first night when she had thrown the tape into the garbage to the night she had come home after Fenton's party and discovered the telltale flowers. Spencer listened like a hawk, frowning and nodding intently every so often, as if he were planning something. Emily was relieved to be able to share it at last.

All week long she'd worked like a demon, setting up a whole new area of his business. She'd hired programmers, checked out job offers and had organized and streamlined his system to maximum efficiency. He'd watched her through all this with admiration that was tinged with amusement. If you want to, then be my guest seemed to be his attitude. She'd even convinced

Spencer to personally oversee the job in Detroit for the following week, but now she had the sickening feeling that it was all about to end, that the whole business she had labored to create would abruptly fold. She should have told him everything in the first place. Now it was too late. She sat there helplessly, watching this extraordinary man trying to think of a way to salvage his life's work, and once again she wanted to crawl into a hole. And yet had it really been all her fault? She was positive that she'd discarded that tape. Someone must have retrieved it. But who?

"I'll just have to do my best to fix it," she said, sighing.

"You can't."

"I can use the negotiating tactics. It was your idea, but I can do it. Just give me the chance."

Suddenly, incongruously, he began to laugh. Boyish peals of laughter spilled around the empty room, growing and increasing as he threw back his head and roared.

"What's so funny?" she asked tonelessly.

"Sometimes, Emily," he said between peals, "this is all there is." He continued laughing with complete abandon, and somehow it was catching. Emily's face began to lighten as she looked at him, and then she was laughing, too, caught in a helpless fit of giggles.

A sudden knock on the door only half sobered them, and the cleaning lady stuck her head inside. "Okay to empty the trash in here?"

Spencer gasped for breath and waved her inside. He turned to Emily, who was choking back her own laughter, and said, "Are you hungry?"

She nodded breathlessly and stood up as the cleaning lady bustled over to the wastebasket and looked inside, singing tunelessly to herself. She clucked her tongue and pulled something out, showing it to them. "A brand-new ashtray," she admonished, shaking her head. "Just 'cause he's the boss, he thinks he can waste things like that." She replaced it on the conference table, next to Fenton's chair. "There, now. That's more like it." She looked self-righteously at Emily and Spencer, who were still chuckling.

"It happens," Spencer said gaily. "Don't worry about it." He and Emily left the room feeling strangely lighthearted, their cares momentarily forgotten. But Emily found that a single, crazy tune kept recurring stubbornly in her head, and try as she might, she couldn't seem to get rid of it. It followed her all the way to the elevator, replaying itself monotonously as they rode down to the lobby. It was the tune that the cleaning lady had been singing.

"Just one of those things . . ." That's exactly right, Emily thought ruefully as they walked onto the street. Just one of those crazy, crazy things.

Chapter Seven

They walked. From the center of Wall Street, Emily and Spencer began a strange odyssey uptown, not sure where they were going and not really caring. All they knew was that they needed to expend energy, to drain themselves of the new problem that had reared its head.

Emily stole a sidelong look at Spencer and saw that he was his usual jaunty self. If he was worried about being sued, he certainly didn't show it. In fact, he seemed to be thinking about something that brought a bona fide smirk to his face from time to time, as if the whole incident had been some kind of practical joke.

As they reached the foot of Greenwich Village, Emily realized that her feet were hot and tired, and yet she didn't want to stop walking. They passed a Spanish restaurant that emanated pleasantly aromatic waves of warm air, and she remembered suddenly that she hadn't had any lunch. She had been too nervous about the board meeting. "It's funny," she said, breaking the silence as they headed up Bleeker Street. "But I have this crazy feeling that nothing is really that wrong." She gave him a tiny smile. "I don't know why."

He smiled back. "Now you're learning."

She nodded slowly, absorbing the new feeling.

"The only way to really be in charge of your life," he said, "is to be able to feel absolutely fine in the face of adversity." He put his arm around her, pulling her close. Emily's heart jumped, but she said nothing, enjoying the warm, solid feel of him lodged against her. He pointed to a tiny Greek restaurant on the corner. "Do you know that they have the best stuffed grape leaves in all of New York there?" he asked. She shook her head. He grinned suddenly as if an idea had just come to him. "Come on." He guided her inside, and a man appeared with menus in his hand.

"I'm interested in your grape leaves," Spencer said directly. "They're the best in New York."

"Thank you," the man said, beaming. "I'll have a table for you in just a moment, if you—"

"No, you don't understand," Spencer interrupted, holding up a hand. He looked at Emily as if she were supposed to understand, but she only gave him a blank look. "Grape leaves," he stated again. "I'd like two."

The man looked perplexed. "Two?"

"That's right. To go." He looked at Emily and smiled, and she returned the smile slowly as she realized what he was doing.

The man shrugged and turned back to the kitchen. A few minutes later, he reappeared holding a small plastic container that held two stuffed grape leaves. Spencer reached for his wallet, but the man held up his hand in refusal. "On the house," he insisted.

Back on the street, they continued to walk uptown. "Say," Emily said with a sudden inspiration, "I know where they make the very best soul food in New York. In the whole world," she corrected herself judiciously. "My father took me there once years ago. Now where was it . . . ?" She thought for a moment, closing her eyes. "Oh, now I remember!" She took him firmly by the arm and led him across town to First Avenue at a brisk trot. They came up to a modest brownstone that didn't look anything like a restaurant, but Emily confidently mounted the steps and rang the bell. A buzzer answered, letting them inside, and they found themselves in a quiet lobby. Still there was no restaurant in sight. They climbed a flight of stairs, and a fantastically dressed black woman met them on the landing. Her head was covered with a brilliant red scarf, gold loops hung from her ears, and a red satin blouse topped a multicolored dirndl skirt that covered her ample hips.

"There ain't no reservations tonight, honey," she drawled. "Sorry." But then her face lit up into a huge smile when she saw who Emily was with. "Why Spencer McIntyre!" she cried. "We ain't seen you in a month of Sundays, honey. Come on in and give me a hug."

Emily was flabbergasted. "You two know each other?" she gaped.

"Of course." Spencer grinned. "The best soul food in New York—or in the whole world, for that matter—couldn't escape me for long."

The woman opened the door, and they could hear the tinkling of a tinny jazz piano coming from inside, mingled with the sound of exuberant voices.

"What's good tonight?" Spencer asked.

"Well, I just cooked up a batch of sweet potato pudding. It's got melted marshmallows on top and—"

"We'll take it," Emily and Spencer said in unison.

"Just a container to go," Spencer added helpfully.

"I can't wait to try it," Emily said when they were walking on First Avenue again.

"We're not finished. Is it my turn again?" Emily's eyes sparkled, and she nodded. "Where to?"

Spencer's choice took them to Ninth Avenue in a taxi, and they stepped out in front of Manganaro's, in the heart of the old Italian neighborhood.

"What's this?" Emily asked curiously.

"Best Italian grocery in America. Come on."

Inside, the small store was brimming with fat cheeses, a hundred different kinds of pasta, salamis hanging on strings, appetizers and pastries. The aromas blended together enticingly, so that Emily's nose crinkled in pleasure the minute they entered. In the back, long wooden tables seated customers who were enjoying large plates of spaghetti.

"What's the best thing here?" Emily asked in wonder. "I don't see how anyone could possibly make a choice."

"You're right," Spencer smirked. "That's why we'll get everything thrown together." As he stepped up to the counter, a burly man wiped his hands on a white apron and looked up. "We'd like a foot-long hero sandwich, please. With everything on it." The man went to work slicing, layering and sprinkling, and they watched his performance in admiration. The long sandwich safely wrapped, they went outside and hailed another cab.

This time they went straight to Little Italy, and the cab deposited them at the head of Mulberry Street. "We need dessert," Spencer announced. Without a word, they both knew exactly where to go. Ferrarra's, the supplier of Italian pastry for all of Little Italy, was crowded as always, but they managed to find a space at the counter where they peered through the glass cases to make their choices.

"I'll have a cannoli," Emily decided after long deliberation.

"Make it two," Spencer agreed, staring hungrily at the pastry tubes stuffed with ricotta cheese and cream.

The pastry was wrapped up in a white box tied with red and white string, and they headed happily onto the street, juggling their packages between them.

"Let's get another cab and go back to my hotel room," Spencer suggested, stepping off the curb to look for an empty taxi.

"No." Emily's tone was vehement, and he looked at her in surprise.

"No?"

"If I have to look at one more empty pizza box, I'm going to scream. I've got a better place."

"Where?" he asked suspiciously.

"You'll see." Emily hailed a cab herself, and they got in. "Take the Brooklyn Bridge to Atlantic Avenue," she said to the driver.

"But where—"

She put a hand on Spencer's arm, silently ordering him to wait, as the cab took off down the narrow street.

They bounced to the southern tip of Manhattan and rolled onto the bridge, its graceful arches rising majestically before them. Then the cab took the turn into Brooklyn Heights, and Emily directed the driver to let them off at the foot of a long walkway. They got out, and Spencer looked around.

"So?" he asked. "What is this?"

She led him onto the walkway, which was lined with benches that faced the harbor, affording a fabulous view of the Statue of Liberty and the southern skyline of Manhattan. "This is the Promenade," she told him, walking briskly. "It's one of Brooklyn's best-kept secrets."

Spencer's eyes were everywhere as they continued to stroll, as if he had to take in the new experience and absorb it immediately. Emily noticed again how full of life he was, how eager to savor each moment. The Promenade was thronged with people who were taking after-work walks, jogging, roller skating and sitting peacefully on the benches. They scurried up and down the long strip, which provided an ever-changing panorama.

Spencer and Emily chose a bench and sat down, carefully unwrapping their bundles. They went through each item one by one, beginning with the savory stuffed grape leaves, which they picked up in their fingers and munched. There was little conversation between them as they went on to the sweet potato pudding, eating it out of the same container with the plastic forks that had been provided. A tugboat chugged by in the harbor, its low whistle letting out a long, lonely sigh. They watched it sail around the tip of Manhattan as they opened the huge hero sandwich, digging in with silent gusto. Emily found the piquant blend of textures and flavors irresistible. The crusty Italian bread was stuffed with smooth provolone and mozarella cheeses and layered with marinated peppers, fresh tomatoes and spicy Italian ham and Genoa salami. It took a long time to make headway through the mountain of the sandwich, but they ate diligently, stopping only to nibble on the olives and mushrooms that had been packed with it.

By the time they got to the cannoli, the sun was low on the horizon, and the crowd on the Promenade had dwindled to a few stragglers. Emily wiped her hands on a paper napkin and leaned back, letting out a long sigh.

"I'm stuffed," she announced, closing her eyes.

"So am I," Spencer said. "Let's leave the cannoli until later."

They cleaned up the debris of the impromptu picnic and sat quietly together, watching as a far-off cargo ship approached from some distant location. Emily could think of nothing to say, because there was nothing left to be said. She had no idea at all what Spencer was thinking. She only knew that she needed him that night, needed to share his strength. He looked contemplative for once, staring out at the ocean, but as always, he remained aloof. So much had happened that it seemed hard to believe he had come into her life only a short time before. It felt as if she had known him for years. Unbidden thoughts of J. P. Fenton and his unleashed wrath invaded her mind, and she tried desperately to push them away. They would have to face the music sooner or later. Emily realized that she was afraid, but she would never admit that to Spencer. He would think her a complete fool. He didn't believe in being afraid of anything—just as he didn't believe in tying himself down to anything.

She looked away, tears brimming suddenly in her eyes. She'd wondered if she could possibly fall in love with a man like Spencer McIntyre, knowing full well the consequences of such a rash and foolish act. And now it was too late. She knew as she sat there next to him, neither one saying a word, that she did love him and that she needed him with a deep and poignant longing that she'd never felt before. Spencer had taught her so much in such a short time. Perhaps he had taught her too much.

"Emily . . ." Spencer broke the peaceful calm.

She looked up. She hoped that he wouldn't become sardonic now. That she couldn't bear. If only he knew how much she needed him, how much she wanted to settle into the comforting shelter of his arms. But he would only laugh at her if she let him know that, so she blinked back her tears and tried to maintain a neutral expression.

"I was wrong about you," he said.

Oh, no. What was this? Was he going to start toying with her again, challenging her to be someone she was not?

"You are very spontaneous," he said quietly. "I should have known. After all, you created Esmerelda."

Despite her gratitude that he was not baiting her for once, Emily groaned. "Please, don't remind me of Esmerelda now."

"Why not? She's your greatest achievement. You should be proud of her."

"She's about to destroy us. I know it."

Spencer lifted his arm and draped it around her shoulders, letting it rest there comfortably. Her heart leaped, but she said nothing, didn't move, for fear of breaking the spell that was weaving around them.

"Emily—" His voice was low and urgent. It was a tone she'd never heard before from him, and it shocked her as much as it thrilled her. "I—" His arm tightened around her, making her shiver slightly in his warm grasp. "I hope you won't think I'm an idiot. But—I think I'm afraid."

She turned to him, her eyes passionate with conviction. "Oh, Spencer!" she cried. Then her head was buried on his shoulder, and he was holding her and rocking her as a wind picked up from the harbor and wafted gently around them. She clung to him blindly, not sure if she was trembling and not really caring. Her feelings had been concealed for so long that it seemed as if they would burst forth suddenly, spilling out recklessly in front of him.

He lifted her head gently and placed a slow, deliberate kiss on her petal-soft lips. The kiss was incredibly comforting, arousing an ancient longing even as it fulfilled her. She opened her mouth slightly, and he accepted the invitation willingly, pressing against her to drink her sweetness and spin them onto a vortex that had no beginning and no end. They kissed again and again, their hands roaming over each other. Emily's eyes were closed as Spencer began a slow, fiery trail across her smooth face and down her slender neck. The brief but tantalizing touches sent a shaft of desire through her, and this time she vowed to herself that nothing would stop them. She needed this man as he needed her. They belonged together; she knew it, and nothing was going to keep them apart. Even if he packed up tomorrow and ran off to Hong Kong, he would always have an irrevocable place in her heart. She knew that she had to have all of him, had to give all of herself before she would know any peace. He was right, as usual. It wasn't Esmerelda at all. It was them.

Now Emily knew that she was trembling, and what was more, Spencer was trembling, too. The knowledge that she aroused him so much thrilled and awed her. So that was the power that could subdue the great Spencer McIntyre! But Emily was in no condition to gloat. She fluttered against him like a small bird, and he crushed her to him, savoring the feel of her slight body molding itself to his hard lines. His lips found hers again with a fever that left her breathless, and his hands strayed restlessly to her sloping shoulders and then to her small breasts. The poignant hunger spread rapidly from the tender peaks of her breasts straight to her loins. His fingers gently grazed the soft mounds, sending shudders of delight coursing through her. She moaned brazenly, no longer caring about what he might think or where they were. Spencer let out a trembling sigh in response, and he drew her to him again and held her close. She wanted to beg him not to stop, but as she opened her eyes reluctantly, she saw people walking on the far end of the Promenade.

"Shall we go?" Spencer whispered. She nodded solemnly and stood up, brushing off her skirt. "Where to?" he asked evenly, as if expecting her to send him home.

"My apartment," she stated firmly. There was nothing else to be said. He took her hand and held it tightly as they walked to the street, quickly traversing the few short blocks to Emily's building.

Their eyes were shining as they approached. Emily could hardly believe it was happening. She had no idea what the next day would bring or what would happen between her and the mercurial man she had come to love. All she knew was that she wanted him as she had never wanted anything in her life.

Chapter Eight

They ran up the one flight to Emily's door, and as she prepared to open it, Spencer suddenly reached down and scooped her up in his arms. She giggled throatily, feeling oddly like a bride, and he took the key from her hand and turned it gently in the lock. He kissed her once before he pushed the door open with his foot and then carried her gracefully inside.

But when he looked around the room and saw who was standing there, he almost dropped her on the floor. A straight, spare figure of a man in military attire stood with his feet planted firmly apart on the carpet, his hands held rigidly behind his back. The two men instantly recognized each other at the same time, neither one hiding his surprise.

"You!" they shouted in unison. Emily looked wildly at the newcomer, and she struggled out of Spencer's grasp. "Stretch!" she cried joyously, but they weren't listening to her.

"What's the matter," the older man said, pointing at Spencer's eyes. "One shiner wasn't enough? Someone else had to teach you a lesson?" His tone was deliberately truculent, and Emily stared at him in astonishment.

"Listen, you old coot," Spencer responded angrily. "I ought to sue you for everything you're—"

"Old coot, eh?" The man charged at Spencer like a

bulldozer, but Emily managed to intervene. He looked at her for the first time and scowled as Spencer hastily retreated. "You know this young hooligan, Emily?" he demanded.

Emily wasn't sure she could handle both of them at once, but she knew she had to try. "Why don't we—" she began, but she got no further.

"Listen, you maniac," Spencer started. "You'd better control yourself."

"For two cents I'd blacken both your eyes, if they weren't already a pair of mud pies." He laughed shortly. "Teach you some manners, you young upstart."

"You and the rest of the army!" Spencer retaliated. "I don't go around hitting old men."

"I am not an old man!" Once again, the colonel tried to get to Spencer, but Emily pushed herself between them forcefully.

"Stop it!" she yelled. "Stop this immediately!" She turned to Spencer and pointed at a chair in the corner of the room. "Sit!" she ordered. "Now!"

Spencer gave the colonel a warning look and then retreated reluctantly to the assigned seat.

"And as for you," she came over to the colonel and kissed him on the cheek. "How are you, dad?"

"Dad!?" Spencer leaped up and stared at both of them in surprise. He touched his two injured eyes ruefully. "I should have realized it. I must be jinxed. There are two of them! Two maniacs loose in New York, and I have to run into both of them. I guess it runs in the family." He sat back down and regarded them sourly. "Something tells me it's going to be a long night."

Emily's father pointed at Spencer. "How long have you known this idiot?" he demanded.

"Take it easy, Dad," she said soothingly. "You know

how hot-tempered you are. Spencer wasn't trying to insult you . . . were you, Spencer?" She turned and threw Spencer a pleading glance.

"No, of course not," he said sarcastically. "It's not every day that an old coot tries to throw me off the Brooklyn Bridge." He pointed at the colonel. "Ask him how close I came to going over the railing. Go ahead, ask him!"

Emily looked at her father. "Is that true?"

"What's the matter, son, can't you swim?" He winked at Emily and laughed. "A dunk in the river might have done you some good. You could use some cooling off."

Spencer was out of his chair again. "You think it's funny?" he shouted. "You could have killed me!"

"If I wanted to kill you, I would have," the colonel said calmly. He turned to Emily. "This young punk thinks he can boss the world around. Imagine, giving me orders! Tells me to get back into my car and wait there like a nice little Boy Scout." This speech got him fired up again, and he strode menacingly toward Spencer all over again. "Boy Scout, is it? I'll show you!" Emily leaped after him and grabbed one of his arms, pinning it behind him in a classic wrestler's hold.

"Ow!" he cried. "Let go!"

"Say uncle!" she commanded.

"No! Let go, I tell you!"

"Say uncle!"

"All right, all right—uncle!"

Emily released her hold, and he straightened up, beaming at her proudly. "I taught you well, didn't I?" he asked. She nodded, a twinkle in her eye. "I guess I'm getting too old for this, though."

She gave him another kiss on the cheek. "You're still as strong as ever, Stretch."

"Stretch?" Spencer asked in spite of himself. "You call your father Stretch?"

The colonel turned to him gruffly. "Where'd you pick this guy up, Emily?"

"I didn't," she said nervously. "He sort of became a coincidence that turned into a business partner."

"Business partner, is it?" Her father looked extremely skeptical. "I've heard of kissing cousins, but this partnership of yours looks more like an invitation to joint custody." He laughed roughly at the joke, but nobody joined him. His shrewd eyes moved back to Spencer. "Community property isn't part of this deal yet, is it?"

"Dad!" Emily scolded. "Spencer and I met about a month ago. Please don't embarrass me. Not yet, anyway."

"Just checking, Em," he said. "Wouldn't want you to make a mistake you'd regret later on." He mussed her hair fondly. "I like that haircut of yours, kid," he added. "Nice and practical." Then he smiled broadly. "So, how'd you give him the other shiner? With that terrific left I taught you?"

Spencer looked from father to daughter like a spectator at a tennis match, as if he couldn't quite believe they were real.

"Leave him alone, Dad," Emily said. "Spencer has had enough trouble from the Moreaus to last him a lifetime." She looked meaningfully at both of them. "Now why don't you two shake hands and make up? We've got enough problems without turning it into a family squabble."

Colonel Moreau laughed boisterously and held out his hand. "Well, son," he said, "I didn't come here to spoil the evening for my daughter. What do you say we call a truce? I've seen enough fighting in my time."

Spencer stared at him quizzically but then got up and shook the man's hand. "You Moreaus have a strange way of showing up at odd times, don't you?" he asked.

"I like to keep people on their toes," the colonel replied heartily.

"Well, sir, I am right up there. On my toes."

The colonel laughed and patted Spencer rigorously on the back.

"Uh—Dad?" Emily broke in. "What are you doing here? I thought you were being transferred to Virginia."

"I am," her father answered, putting his other arm around her. He tried to smile at both of them, but Emily knew him better than that and frowned searchingly.

"What is it, Dad? Come on, I know you too well. What is it?"

"Well, Em," he said, the grin fading. He dropped his arms and walked over to the chair that Spencer had occupied. He looked much older suddenly, and Emily's heart skipped a beat. He motioned for the two of them to sit down also, and they did, leaving a safe gap between them on the couch. "Emily," he began again, and his face began to sag. She took a deep breath and waited. "They gave me the boot." He threw up his hands and heaved a long sigh. "After forty-seven years of service. Can you imagine that? Funny"—he chuckled bravely—"I've seen all kind of action, and nothing ever fazed me. But now they're retiring me and putting me out to pasture, and I have to admit, it feels kind of bad."

No one said anything for a long minute as they contemplated the effects of what the colonel had said. Finally, Spencer spoke. "You've got the rest of your life still in front of you."

"Listen, son," the colonel said. "You don't have to

tell me that." He looked at his daughter and smiled a little. "I didn't come here to cry on anyone's shoulder. I just came to announce that I'm starting a new life. Only I don't know where, and I'm not sure how." He smiled again, gamely this time, and Emily's chin lifted. "Got any ideas?"

Spencer looked at the older man with admiration, and Emily said wryly, "You came to the right place. Spencer here should have lots of good ideas. He's an expert at leisure activities."

"That's true," Spencer said, completely missing her gentle needling. "Now from the way it sounds, you've had enough of traveling, is that correct?"

The colonel nodded. "You know, there's a little farm for sale in the area where I first met Mrs. Moreau, back when I was on leave after the big one." He stopped and thought back for a moment. "I always wanted to go back there with her after I had had enough of army life. But I guess when I lost her, the army was the best place for me to be." He smiled nostalgically and looked at Emily. "I really took you all over with me, didn't I, kid?"

"I have no complaints," Emily said sincerely. "I loved every minute of it."

"She's a good little soldier," the colonel said staunchly.

"Rank and file," Spencer added, not looking at her.

Emily ignored him and sighed. "Well," she said, "I think we could all use a good strong cup of coffee right about now." She stood up and headed for the kitchen.

"You might think about putting something a little stronger in it," her father called after her. "Like a nice shot of bourbon."

Emily smiled knowingly and went to put the coffee on, hunting in the cabinet for the old bottle of bourbon she had bought the last time her father was there. The living room was quiet, and she breathed a silent prayer of relief that the tiff was over. She knew well how hot-tempered her father could be. And Spencer—she wasn't sure she understood him at all.

It was funny how things turned out. First the Fenton catastrophe and now her father's unexpected retirement. It seemed such a shame that good people could get booted out or "retired." Surely the world could use a little less paper work and more humane, common sense. As she started the coffee perking, she could hear the voices in the living room talking reasonably. Then, to her surprise, the conversation was followed by loud laughter. It grew louder and more raucous, punctuated by occasional hoots and her father's familiar guffaws. She hurried back into the room curiously and saw the two of them howling with laughter and slapping each other on the back.

"Do you know what this character did to an army defense computer?" her father asked as he burst into a fresh peal of laughter.

"I accidentally mixed up a program," Spencer said.

"Mixed up?" her father repeated. "I'll say! He managed to send forty transport planes zooming over Virginia. Ten thousand men parachuted down into the cornfields before anyone knew what was happening."

Emily lifted an eyebrow and looked pointedly at Spencer.

"I didn't know the machine was connected to the main command terminal," he explained sheepishly. "I was playing around with a mock battle, and I ended up sending parachuters to attack Virginia."

The two men burst out laughing again, and Emily shook her head ruefully. It was nice to see the two of them getting along so well, but she had the feeling that the night would still be full of surprises. She turned around and headed back to the kitchen when a scribbled note by the telephone caught her eye. She read it once, twice, and then slowly put the coffeepot down with shaking hands.

"Uh—Dad . . . ?" she asked in such a sober voice that they stopped laughing and looked at her. "When did Mr. Fenton call?"

Spencer's face changed rapidly as he grabbed the note out of her hand. As he read it, the colonel was off on a new tirade. "Oh, that. That was a real upstart on the phone. A card-carrying hooligan. He threatened to peel my ears back, the bum."

Emily and Spencer looked at each other, their faces gray. "Uh . . . Mr. Moreau?" Spencer said.

"Call me Stretch."

"Stretch," Spencer said urgently. "What exactly did Fenton say?"

"Him? Oh, something about me being a possible conspirator in a crime. And something about a girl friend snitching." His face became angry. "I didn't understand a word he said, but he owes me an apology. I don't like being talked to in that tone of voice, and I don't like hooligans calling up my daughter and—"

"His girl friend?" Emily broke in. "Dad, think. Did he mention the girl friend's name?" Her voice was trembling.

Her father put his hand to his chin. "Well, let me see. Come to think of it, he said it was . . . Ethel. No, that's not it. It was something like that. Oh, now I remember. Esmerelda! Yes, he said he went right to the horse's mouth and asked her point-blank." He looked at both their faces drop. "Hey, now, kids, it can't be all that bad. Don't worry, I gave that guy a real piece of my mind. He was a real horse's—"

"Dad?" Emily asked, panic-stricken. "Did he say anything else?"

Spencer was leaning forward anxiously. "Please, Stretch. Did he say anything else?"

"Uh, no, not that I recall. He was in a big hurry. I simply called him an appropriate name, and we hung up."

Emily felt a lead weight in the pit of her stomach, and she sat down heavily. "We're in trouble," she announced. "Big trouble." She let out a long, shaky sigh. "He knows."

"Knows what?" her father asked bluntly. "Who knows?"

She looked at Spencer, and he nodded once. As briefly as possible, she told her father the whole story, starting with the day she was fired and continuing right up to their latest efforts to remove Esmerelda from the computer. He nodded vigorously several times and laughed appreciatively at the poems and the flowers that had been sent to the terminated employees.

"Not bad," he said. "The army didn't even give me a gold watch."

"But that's not all," Spencer said. "We are going to be held responsible for everything."

"I see," the colonel said grimly, nodding to himself. "Well, it looks like this is a bad night for all of us."

"It could be the end for us," Emily said wretchedly. "I can just see the lawsuit. And all because I—"

"Now wait just a minute here, Em," her father said commandingly, standing up to his full height. "No one has said anything about a lawsuit here. From what you tell me, this Esmerelda sounds like quite a gal. You may have created her, but you didn't put her into that system."

"Yes, but Fenton won't believe that," Emily started to say impatiently, but her father held up a hand.

"Maybe not. But what you've got to do now is to find

the upstart that did it. Someone put that tape into the system, and that someone can be found. Once you accomplish that, your problems are over."

"Our problems are just beginning," Spencer said.

"Why don't you talk to the old coot?" the colonel suggested, making Spencer smirk behind his hand. "This Fenton character can't be a total fool if he's president of the company." He frowned for a moment, thinking. "I'll just bet that the real culprit is right up there alongside Fenton." Emily looked up in surprise. "Sure," he continued, warming to his lead. "You say that only Fenton has the top access code to get inside that contraption, right?" They both nodded avidly. "Then it had to be someone close to the boss. Someone who was able to get that code." He continued to think to himself as the doorbell rang.

Emily got up to answer it, and without thinking, she swung open the door. A messenger was standing there with a telegram. It was addressed to McIntyre, Inc. in care of Emily Moreau. Her heart dropped when she saw it, but she signed the receipt shakily and carried the telegram into the living room as though it were a bomb. Dropping it wordlessly onto the coffee table, she gestured silently at it and sank down into a chair.

Spencer picked it up and ripped it open. He read it quickly, his expression dark. Emily waited in suspense, the seconds passing like lengthy minutes.

At last, Spencer looked up. "It's from Esmerelda," he said, handing it to her. She read it fearfully, turned pale and dropped it down again, letting her head fall into her hands. Her father snatched it up curiously and read it aloud.

I SUPPOSE YOU THOUGHT IT WAS VERY FUNNY,

PLANNING A FELONY WITH YOUR HONEY.
TO SHOW YOU HOW DELIGHTED HE IS WITH
YOUR MIRTH,
FENTON IS SUING FOR ALL YOU'RE WORTH.
                              LOVE,
                              ESMERELDA

"Oh, God," Emily groaned, standing up and then sitting down again. "Oh, my God."

Spencer leaped up and began to pace the room like a caged tiger. Finally, he collapsed on the arm of the sofa, mumbling something about a job in South America.

The colonel got up and came over to him, patting him roughly on the shoulder. "Son," he said sternly in his best military style, "there comes a time in every man's life when he is faced with a great hardship. This situation seems to be one of those times, and you've got to handle it like a man." He paused, looking Spencer straight in the eye. "There's only one manly thing to do in the face of such adversity."

Chapter Nine

"Bottoms up!" Spencer raised the first shot of bourbon that the waiter had brought, and Emily and the colonel followed suit.

"Look out, stomach!" Emily said.

They all downed their first shot, Emily shuddering at the sting it gave her. "Phew!" she said as her father poured another round. "I felt something loosen up down there."

"Just the beginning, Em. I've been known to drink four-star generals under the table. Tonight I intend to wind up there myself." He raised the second glass. "Here's to heartless electronic dictators!"

"To Esmerelda, the snitch," Emily added.

"To poetic license," Spencer joined in. "Esmerelda's, that is."

They all downed another round and then sat back and waited for the inevitable effect to hit them.

"What are we celebrating here?" the waiter asked congenially.

"Transitions," Spencer answered for all of them. He stole a glance at Emily. "And partnerships, right?"

"For good or bad," she agreed.

"For richer or for poorer," Spencer said. "Till death do us part."

"Oh, I see," the waiter nodded as he refilled their glasses. "You're tying one on, right?"

"That's right," Emily said. "We're going to tie on a big one, and why not?"

"Why not?" her father repeated. "I remember the last time I tied one on. It was with General Bradford in the Philippines. The old goat was—"

"No, no," the waiter broke in. "I didn't mean tie one on as in getting drunk."

They all looked at him. "Well, whatever in tarnation did you mean?" the colonel asked.

"I was talking about tying knots, not—" He looked at Emily, who had straightened suddenly in her chair. "I mean—well, you were talking about partnerships, richer and poorer and all that."

"Right," Spencer rejoined. He lifted his third glass and saluted. "For richer or for poorer. Whatever comes along. We'll face the music together."

The third shot went down easily, and Emily wondered nervously if her two companions realized that the waiter had been talking about a different kind of partnership.

"Do you know what this nice young lady did?" Spencer drawled, looping his arm around Emily's shoulders. His touch sent a little tingle through her, but she didn't move. The waiter listened with indulgent interest. "She took a perfectly normal electronic machine and gave it a brain." The waiter nodded politely, and Spencer suddenly dropped his arm and began to curl his hands together in the style of an evil demon in a grade D horror movie. "She gave it a human brain, complete with emotions. She created a new Frankenstein!" He quickly poured another round and lifted his glass. "To Esmerelda!" he toasted, and they all swallowed in unison.

Emily almost gagged. "Argh!" she cried. "I think something just happened to my equilibrarian."

"That's equilibrium," Spencer corrected mildly. "I think."

"Whatever. Something in me just closed down for the night."

"It's good for you," her father said gruffly. He was still speaking clearly, but Emily and Spencer were both decidedly glazed.

Spencer looked at the colonel admiringly. "How do you do it?" he asked. "Four shots of bourbon and you look like you could dance an Irish jig."

"I could, son. But Emily can top that easily, can't you, kid?" He looked at his daughter with one raised eyebrow.

"Oh, no, Dad, please. Not tonight. Not ever, but especially not tonight."

"Why not?" her father demanded. "I say it's the perfect time. Go on, girl. Get out on that floor, and I'll see if that old piano in the corner can still shake a leg."

"It can," the waiter confirmed helpfully.

"Good!" The colonel marched over to the battered old piano and seated himself briskly on the bench. His fingers danced expertly over the keys as he warmed up with a few scales.

"Hey, not bad," Spencer remarked. "Where did you learn to play like that?"

"I taught him," Emily said darkly. "The biggest mistake of my life."

"Come on, Em!" her father called out as he launched into a spirited rendition of "Alexander's Ragtime Band." "Show them what you can do!" He looked at the other patrons, who were watching with amused interest. There weren't many people there, and he was able to rouse them into a response. Some of them began to applaud encouragingly. "Get out here, Em!" he called, and then turned back to his audience. "She used to dance on 'Uncle Bernie's Children's Hour,'" he explained proudly.

"Uncle Ernie's," Emily corrected sheepishly. "And it was only for half a season." Spencer was grinning wickedly at her, no help at all. She had no choice but to stand up and wobble her way to the center of the floor. The patrons applauded enthusiastically. She was quite dizzy, but as her father continued playing, her feet began to move. With lightning speed, she began a tap that sounded like a drum roll. Faster and faster she went until she couldn't see straight, and then she threw her arms out in a show-biz gesture that meant, "That's all, folks!" But her father wasn't ready to let her quit, and he grabbed her arm before she could stagger back to the table.

"Now, come on, girl, show these folks what you're made of. 'Tea for Two,' key of D."

"Forget it," she protested. "That is too corny. I absolutely refuse."

But to Spencer's vast amusement, her father persisted, singing coaxingly in his bullish voice as he played. "'Tea for two, and two for me'. . . . Move it, Em! Let me see those feet fly!" he hollered. "'You and me, and me for you' . . . this minute, and that's an order!"

"Yes, sir!" Emily saluted, deciding to make the best of an embarrassing situation. She broke into the fanciest footwork of which she was capable in her present condition, tapping up a storm on the tavern floor.

The place broke into appreciative laughter and applause, and she managed to finish out the song. Then she hobbled back to the table, collapsing gratefully next to Spencer. "No more!" she gasped. "I'm not in shape."

"That was terrific," Spencer said with drunken enthusiasm. He pulled her onto his lap and, without warning, gave her a long, lush kiss that left her breathless. Emily scarcely knew what to do, but she wasn't sure she could muster up the energy to care. Spencer was kissing her passionately there in the tavern, in front of her father, in front of the waiter, in front of everybody, and all she really wanted to do was to kiss him back with all her heart.

"Careful, son!" her father called out, breaking the spell. "You'd better have good intentions!"

"I'm an officer and a gentleman, I assure you, sir," Spencer answered gallantly.

Emily picked up the bottle and poured another drink. She struggled out of Spencer's grasp and brought the drink over to her father. "Here you go, Dad," she said, bending down to kiss his cheek.

"What was that for?" he asked.

"I don't want you to feel left out."

He launched into a loud version of "Get Me to the Church on Time." "You know, Em," he said, picking up the glass. He downed the drink in one shot before continuing. "That's quite a guy you've got there." Emily said nothing. "I'm sorry I hit him so hard. He's got spunk. And independence, too. Am I right?" Emily remained silent, wondering desperately if Spencer could hear what her father was saying. "You don't have to answer," he went on. "I know a good thing when I see it. That's one tough soldier over there. I bet he threw away the book before he ever read it."

Emily couldn't help but laugh. "Actually, he wrote his own."

"Well, I'm not surprised," he said as he went into the chorus. His hands pounded the keys forcefully, and he didn't look up as he finished what he wanted to say. "He certainly is crazy about you." Emily almost jumped. "I can tell a mile away. I've been in charge of enough platoons to know all the signs. That guy's got nothing but you on his mind." He peered around Emily to sneak a look at Spencer. "See what I mean? He can't take his eyes off you."

Emily's mind darted back to the scene on the Promenade, and suddenly she wondered exactly what would have happened if her father hadn't made his untimely appearance. She'd been expecting a no-strings evening, but perhaps Spencer had been prepared to offer more —much more. Her heart fluttered a little, and she caught Spencer's eye. Leaving her father to finish banging out the song, she went back to the table and sat down next to Spencer, feeling pleasantly woozy but strangely alert.

The waiter glided over and obligingly poured the last of the bourbon into their glasses. He tipped the bottle upside down and shook it a few times, letting the last few drops empty out.

"That's it, folks," he said cheerfully. "All gone."

Spencer bravely raised his glass. "To—to chance!" he cried. "To all the crazy things that happen in life."

"All the crazy things," Emily repeated, slurring the words slightly. "All the crazy, crazy things."

Spencer quickly downed his drink, but when he looked up, Emily's was still sitting on the table, untouched.

"'Just one of those things,'" she was mumbling to herself.

"What's the matter, Emily?" he asked, leaning forward. "Go on. Drink up."

But Emily still hadn't moved. "'Just one of those crazy, crazy things,'" she sang shakily.

"Careful!" the colonel called out. "I think she's going to topple over."

"No, I'm not," Emily said, looking up earnestly. "I'm not going to fall." She looked at Spencer and laughed suddenly, sounding happier than she had felt all day. "I've found it!" she said, beaming. "I've found the missing tape." She threw back her head and laughed wildly. "It's just one of those crazy things!"

Spencer stared at her, and then his face broke in comprehension. "The cleaning lady!" he cried. "Of course—and right in front of our noses. Let's go." He stood up, holding onto the edge of the table for support.

"Where to?" the colonel asked as he finished the song.

"The Fenton Building. Wall Street. We just found Esmerelda's brain."

Chapter Ten

"And so we've found the culprit," Emily said earnestly to J. P. Fenton.

Fenton looked at her skeptically, and she winced a little from the sunlight that was streaming in through the office window. She and Spencer were both suffering from severe hangovers, but they'd managed to drag themselves there for an all-important interview. Emily could only dimly remember what had transpired the night before after they had left the bar. The three of them had stumbled into a cab and had gone directly to the Fenton Building, where Spencer had led them to the terminal room. And there they had uncovered the priceless, elusive tape that had turned Esmerelda into a reality.

It had been so simple, once they had seen it. Florence Luchek, the cleaning woman, had found the tape in the trash can and had placed it haphazardly on a shelf. What she couldn't have known was that she randomly chose the shelf that held newly created programs awaiting executive approval to be transferred permanently into the system.

"So you see," Emily finished, "it was all a terrible, unfortunate coincidence."

"You admit you're the one who created Esmerelda?"

Fenton growled. She nodded bravely. "You made a mockery of my company?"

"Oh, no, sir," she said hastily. "I—I was just . . . experimenting."

Fenton sat back, his eyes narrowed, studying both of them. "It's a good thing I finally had the sense to ask that idiotic Esmerelda herself who had created her. She supplied the answer with no hesitation whatsoever." Emily and Spencer exchanged a brief, regretful glance that was not lost on Fenton. "Didn't think you'd get caught, did you?"

Emily sighed, fighting back her headache. "Yes, we did. We were about to tell you ourselves when we got the telegram."

Fenton leaned forward aggressively. "And you expect me to swallow all of this? A cleaning woman is responsible, and you're not?" His voice grew louder as he continued. "You were about to come to me and confess? Hah!"

"Shhh!" Spencer's hand flew to his forehead. "Not so loud. My head is on fire."

"I must repeat," Emily said emphatically, "the cleaning woman is not to blame, and neither are we. The person who signed the authorization for that tape to go into the system is the real culprit."

"And who would be stupid enough to do that?" Fenton demanded.

Emily held up the crucial tape. "There are no notations at all on the reel. It could have been anything, for all anyone knew."

"You mean to tell me that someone in this company actually put their okay on this tape to go into the computer?"

Emily and Spencer both nodded vigorously at the same time.

"And who, may I ask, was that?"

Emily cleared her throat. "Uh—it was you, sir." She pointed to the hastily scrawled initials on the back of the tape. "See for yourself."

Fenton grabbed the tape in astonishment and examined it avidly. "My initials," he confirmed in wonder. "Are you telling me that I accidentally sabotaged my own operations?" He still sounded as if he were accusing them, but Emily was no longer nervous.

"It certainly appears that way, sir," she said as evenly as she could manage.

Fenton sat back in his chair and thought it all over for a long minute. Then he threw back his head and began to laugh uproariously. Emily smiled politely and Spencer continued to hold his head in one hand. Fenton laughed for a long time, and they sat patiently and waited for him to stop. When he did, Spencer let his hand drop, and he looked up.

"Now that we've got that tape," he said, "it will be a cinch to remove Esmerelda completely from the system. The tape is the blueprint of the entire program."

"That's right," Emily added eagerly. "In less than a week, we can have you back to—"

"Forget it." Fenton spoke abruptly, and they looked up at him in utter surprise. "I can't take that chance."

"What chance?" Emily asked. "As Spencer explained, there is no longer the slightest risk involved. Now that we have the original tape, we can remove Esmerelda piece by piece."

"No, thanks." Fenton got up and walked to the door, turning once to throw Emily a curiously friendly smile.

"Tell me, Fenton." It was Spencer, looking as if he knew something that Emily didn't. "How much?"

Emily looked at him, wondering what he meant, but he wasn't looking at her. He was watching Fenton confidently, waiting for an answer.

Fenton transferred the smile to Spencer. "Seventeen percent," he said conspiratorially. And then he was gone.

Spencer nodded to himself, obviously very satisfied about something. He began to chuckle quietly, mumbling, "Well, I'll be."

"Would you mind telling me what that was all about?" Emily asked him finally. She was bursting with curiosity.

Spencer smiled at her, his face radiating with a happiness she hadn't seen since the day they had spent on the beach. "Fenton International Industries went up seventeen percent in profits this month," he explained. "And all because of our girl friend here." He patted the tape fondly. "My guess is that people are actually working more productively because the computer is such a novelty. And the coffee breaks and all the rest of it are not against production at all. They're actually designed to enhance it." He laughed quietly. "I suspect that Fenton didn't like being made a fool of—the poetry and all the rest of it was highly embarrassing to him. But he's an old tycoon, and he's still a good businessman. When profits go up this much, you don't argue. He'll be laughing all the way to the bank."

Emily digested all of it and realized that a terrible, oppressive weight had just been lifted from her shoulders. The realization came slowly, in gentle layers, and when it had completely sunk in, she fell back in her chair and let out a long sigh of sheer relief.

"I can't believe it," she said wondrously. "And I was so worried."

"You see, Emily? It all worked out."

They looked at each other, and suddenly they both burst out laughing, all of the tension dissolved. Their laughter built into a crescendo, died down and then abruptly erupted again, until they were both slapping the sides of their chairs and bending over with mirth. "To think," Emily gasped, "that Fenton International Industries will be ruled by Esmerelda forever!"

"It's the damndest thing I've ever seen," Spencer agreed, "but Fenton knows a good thing when he sees it." They kept laughing until they were exhausted, and suddenly a weighty silence fell between them.

"Well," Emily said.

"Well," Spencer repeated after a pause.

"Uh—I guess this job is over now."

"I guess it is."

Emily looked down at her lap, keenly aware that the future loomed before them, and she wasn't at all sure what it would hold. Now that the crushing problem at Fenton was solved, she and Spencer would have to come to terms with what had been developing between them since they had met. And suddenly she wasn't so sure she wanted to do that. Spencer would undoubtedly return to his nomadic, episodic life style, and she knew better than to expect miracles from him. He was too much his own man. He would expect her to be just as spontaneous and independent as he always was himself.

"Uh—" she tried again, looking up cautiously. "It's back to business as usual."

"Yes."

He was being no help at all. She would have to take the initiative. "Well," she said with sudden briskness, "I'll be flying to California, and you'll have to go to Tokoyo, after all. They're having a problem there that only you can handle."

"What? I am?" For the first time, Spencer seemed interested. "And what's in California?"

"Our new client. I forgot to tell you. I took on a new job that was such a plum I couldn't say no. It will only take a week, and I'm sure I can manage it." She said it all very quickly, and Spencer didn't look pleased at all. She had no idea what he was thinking, except that he seemed suddenly very bored with the whole thing. "You don't mind, do you?" she asked, thinking that he might want to be kept informed of new assignments.

"Mind?" he answered dully. "Oh . . . no, no. Go right ahead."

"Good," she said uncertainly. "Well, then, I guess I'll just make all the travel arrangements and be on my way."

"Emily . . ." There was something in his eyes that had never been there before, and she leaped at the spark that she hoped was there.

"Yes?" she said quickly.

There was a long pause. "Uh, nothing. Have a good trip."

That did it. She stood up and brushed at her skirt self-consciously. "Would you like me to take care of your plane tickets for Japan?"

"What? Oh, sure. That would be fine."

She could think of absolutely nothing else to say, but she stood there, anyway, staring at him meaningfully. Ask me to stay, dammit, her mind insisted. Go ahead, ask me. She willed him silently to respond, to show some sign that he cared, but he only nodded at her pleasantly. She was dying inside.

There was nothing to do except leave. She forced herself to walk to the door with as much outward calm as she could manage. "Good-bye, Spencer," she said softly.

"Good-bye, Emily. Have a nice trip."

She turned and left without looking back.

Emily buckled her seat belt and stared out the window at the blank landscape of the airport. She'd found herself booked on that flight before she quite knew what was happening, and there had been nothing to do but pack and resolve to go on with the new life she'd created for herself.

But it was a very hollow victory. She had won a full partnership in McIntyre, Inc., but she was well aware that she would see Spencer rarely, if ever. He was hardly ever around. Whatever his feelings for her had been, they obviously had not been strong enough to make him change his singular way of living. She knew she could never live like that, and she also knew that it was better for her to have found out when she did. But that was poor consolation as she thumbed listlessly through the airline magazine and waited for the flight to take off.

The passengers filed slowly on the plane, toting their small pieces of luggage and personal paraphernalia. Emily had the feeling that it was going to be a long, long flight. The sky outside was a dull gray, matching her spirits. She closed her eyes in a vain attempt to shut out the world around her.

"Hi." The sound of someone taking the seat next to her caused her eyes to fly open.

"Spencer!" She almost fell out of her seat. "What are you doing here?"

He looked at her with that smug calm she had come to know so well. "I'm flying to California."

"But—but you're supposed to go to Japan! I made the reservation myself. They're expecting you, Spencer. You can't just—"

"I know," he interrupted coolly. "I changed it. I told them I'd come next week instead. With you."

"With me!"

"With you. You have some objection?" he asked, arching an eyebrow.

"Well . . . no, but why are you going to California?"

Her voice was raised to a squeaky pitch in astonishment.

"Stop acting so shocked, Emily. What did you expect me to do?" His cool tone was maddening.

"I expected you to go to Japan!" she retorted, almost shouting. "What are you doing here?"

"Well, I—" He dried up suddenly, the jaunty manner disappearing into thin air.

Emily began to suspect something that hadn't occurred to her before. "Spencer," she said slowly, "are you . . . shy?"

His head jerked up. "Me? Shy?" Then his face fell. "Yes, as a matter of fact. How did you guess?"

She began to smile a little, and the cloud of despondency that had enveloped her before vanished. Her heart was beating rapidly in anticipation, and she had a sure instinct that she was about to become extremely, impossibly happy. "I'm shy, too," she confided softly. "Maybe we're both too shy."

He nodded. "Then one of us will have to break the ice."

She looked at him warmly. "Any volunteers?"

He looked into her eyes for a long moment that lasted for a small eternity. "I volunteer," he whispered at last. "You know why I'm here, don't you, Emily?" She started to look down again, but he caught her chin with one finger and held it. "I love you, Emily. And I need you. I came to find out if we have a future together."

The happiness that she had been anticipating swelled up in her like a sunburst, and she knew that her face was radiating her joy. She didn't have to say a word. The heart-stopping look of love on her face said it all. They kissed, briefly at first, and then with the heady passion that had been fired by their precious discovery. Spencer enfolded her in his arms, crushing her against him fiercely. For several minutes, neither of them said a word as they nestled together, listening to the beating of their own hearts.

It was Spencer who broke the magical silence. "To think that we owe all of this to Esmerelda." She nodded, still too happy for words. "Maybe we should offer an Esmerelda package to all of our clients," he continued. "We could start a whole new trend. I left some notes back in my room at the Waldorf that you might want to look at. If I go to Detroit next week, you can come with me, and we'll work on it there." He smiled. "You'll love the hotel there, Em. My room has this great—"

Emily sat up. "Wait a minute," she said.

"What is it?"

"I don't want to hear about your hotel room in Detroit." A terrible fear was gnawing at her, but she had to find out. It was what she had feared all along. "Where else do you have hotel rooms?"

"Houston. L.A. London. A few others. They're all terrific. Why?"

Emily closed her eyes and shook her head. "No," she said in a low but clear voice. "Forget it, Spencer."

"What are you talking about?"

She opened her eyes and looked at him, wincing as she realized how much she loved him. But something was missing. Something very crucial and necessary. "I'm sorry," she said slowly. It was the hardest thing she had ever had to say in her life. "I—I can't go with you."

"Why not?"

"It's not for me," she said as kindly as she could. "I'm still an old-fashioned girl, Spencer. I can't help that, and I don't want to change it. Call it rank and file if you like, but that's how I am. I can't go chasing around with you from hotel room to hotel room, always on the run. I can't have a life full of crazy restaurants and card games and empty pizza boxes and—"

"But I'm not asking you to do all that," he broke in.

"Yes, you are," she insisted. "And I'm not buying it." She turned around in her seat to face him, her eyes blazing. "When are you going to grow up, Spencer? When are you going to settle down and make a real life for yourself?"

"I am!" he exploded, grasping her arms with both hands. "I'm asking you to marry me!"

She was stunned. "You are?" It sounded ridiculously stupid, and for a moment they could only stare at each other dumbly.

"Of course," he said finally. "What did you think I was asking?"

She found her voice. "To—to just live like a nomad. To run from hotel to hotel. To . . ." She ran out of words altogether.

"Emily," he said with a new note of authority. "I want you to listen to me. No, don't interrupt. We are going to fly to California, and we are going to tackle the job out there. Then we are going to go back to New York, and we are going to find a place to live. A permanent place with a real address. And then we are going to get married. Did you get all that?"

She nodded. "But what about—?"

"What about what? The hotel rooms? I'll get rid of them." He put his arms around her, letting his hands settle intimately around the back of her neck. "You've taught me a great deal, Emily. I wouldn't admit it before because I was too stubborn. Or too blind." He smiled. "Or too shy. But you're right. I can't keep hiding out in strange places. People who do that have a way of growing old too fast, with no one around for company."

Emily could feel the incredible happiness beginning

its slow journey again, but she didn't quite trust it yet. "Tell me something, Spencer," she said. "Are you saying all this only because you think it's what I want to hear?"

"Yes," he answered promptly, and her heart took a nosedive. "I'm saying this just to whisk you to the altar, but I'll be laughing the whole time. I'm going to change my life and get a real place to live just for the fun of it." His face changed, and he flushed with a sudden anger. It was the first time she had really seen him angry, and it frightened her. "I'm baring my soul to you, Emily Moreau. Why do you question me? Don't you think I know what I'm doing? I fell in love with you, and I want to share my life with you. Say yes, dammit."

She shut her eyes tight. "Yes," she said very quickly.

"Yes?" The change in him was so sudden that it was almost comical. He looked as if he could scarcely believe it.

"Yes," she repeated softly, looking into his eyes. "What's the matter, McIntyre? Getting cold feet already?" The tiny trace of a smile was flirting around her mouth.

"No," he whispered solemnly. "I had cold feet for too long." A crazy smile lit up his face. "Now I have hot feet."

Emily giggled. "Me, too." They kissed for a long, full minute. Emily was lost in his arms, filled with a delicious sense of surrender as he slowly explored her mouth with his tongue. Her head fell back as he claimed her, letting him work his magic. He covered her face with countless smaller kisses and left a feverish trail down the side of her neck that made her shiver.

Suddenly, they were aware of a large jolt, and they opened their eyes reluctantly and looked around. The plane had just taken off and was lifting gracefully into the sky. They watched wordlessly for a moment as the tops of the trees disappeared and the plane climbed higher and higher, finally surfacing through the clouds. Then they turned back to each other.

"Dad is going to be so happy," Emily said.

"Stretch," he said. "My father-in-law. That's quite a prospect."

He started to kiss her again, but this time they were interrupted by the arrival of a flight attendant.

"Mr. McIntyre?" she asked in a friendly voice.

Spencer turned around. "Yes?"

"This is for you and Ms. Moreau." The young woman held out a brightly wrapped package addressed to Emily and Spencer in care of McIntyre, Inc. "It arrived just before takeoff." She smiled brightly and handed it to him.

"What is it?" Emily asked curiously. "And who sent it?"

"I don't know. There's a card, though." The flight attendant pointed to a small white envelope stapled neatly to the paper, smiled again and left, trotting back up the aisle.

Emily looked at the package, consumed with curiosity. "I'm almost afraid to open it," she said.

"I'll do the honors." Spencer held the package firmly and carefully tore away the paper. Inside, there was a bottle of very old, very rare champagne.

"Wow" was Emily's first comment. "But who's it from? Open the card."

He ripped open the envelope obligingly and pulled out the card. His eyes scanned it quickly, and then he burst out laughing.

"What is it?" she demanded. "Give me that."

"I should have known." he chuckled, shaking his head. "Who else?"

Emily grabbed the card and looked at it. It was neatly printed with a short message.

HERE'S FROM FENTON'S PRIVATE STOCK,
I DON'T THINK THAT HE'LL MISS IT,
AND EVEN IF HE DID FIND OUT,
I'M SURE HE WOULD DISMISS IT.
FOR GOOD OLD J.P. WOULD HAVE TO AGREE
THAT PEOPLE LIKE YOU ARE RARE.
ENJOY YOUR TRIP AND HAVE A SIP
AND DON'T FORGET TO SHARE!

LOVE,
ESMERELDA

Silhouette Romance

IT'S YOUR OWN SPECIAL TIME
Contemporary romances for today's women.
Each month, six very special love stories will be yours
from SILHOUETTE.

$1.75 each

☐ 100 Stanford	☐ 127 Roberts	☐ 155 Hampson	☐ 182 Clay
☐ 101 Hardy	☐ 128 Hampson	☐ 156 Sawyer	☐ 183 Stanley
☐ 102 Hastings	☐ 129 Converse	☐ 157 Vitek	☐ 184 Hardy
☐ 103 Cork	☐ 130 Hardy	☐ 158 Reynolds	☐ 185 Hampson
☐ 104 Vitek	☐ 131 Stanford	☐ 159 Tracy	☐ 186 Howard
☐ 105 Eden	☐ 132 Wisdom	☐ 160 Hampson	☐ 187 Scott
☐ 106 Dailey	☐ 133 Rowe	☐ 161 Trent	☐ 188 Cork
☐ 107 Bright	☐ 134 Charles	☐ 162 Ashby	☐ 189 Stephens
☐ 108 Hampson	☐ 135 Logan	☐ 163 Roberts	☐ 190 Hampson
☐ 109 Vernon	☐ 136 Hampson	☐ 164 Browning	☐ 191 Browning
☐ 110 Trent	☐ 137 Hunter	☐ 165 Young	☐ 192 John
☐ 111 South	☐ 138 Wilson	☐ 166 Wisdom	☐ 193 Trent
☐ 112 Stanford	☐ 139 Vitek	☐ 167 Hunter	☐ 194 Barry
☐ 113 Browning	☐ 140 Erskine	☐ 168 Carr	☐ 195 Dailey
☐ 114 Michaels	☐ 142 Browning	☐ 169 Scott	☐ 196 Hampson
☐ 115 John	☐ 143 Roberts	☐ 170 Ripy	☐ 197 Summers
☐ 116 Lindley	☐ 144 Goforth	☐ 171 Hill	☐ 198 Hunter
☐ 117 Scott	☐ 145 Hope	☐ 172 Browning	☐ 199 Roberts
☐ 118 Dailey	☐ 146 Michaels	☐ 173 Camp	☐ 200 Lloyd
☐ 119 Hampson	☐ 147 Hampson	☐ 174 Sinclair	☐ 201 Starr
☐ 120 Carroll	☐ 148 Cork	☐ 175 Jarrett	☐ 202 Hampson
☐ 121 Langan	☐ 149 Saunders	☐ 176 Vitek	☐ 203 Browning
☐ 122 Scofield	☐ 150 Major	☐ 177 Dailey	☐ 204 Carroll
☐ 123 Sinclair	☐ 151 Hampson	☐ 178 Hampson	☐ 205 Maxam
☐ 124 Beckman	☐ 152 Halston	☐ 179 Beckman	☐ 206 Manning
☐ 125 Bright	☐ 153 Dailey	☐ 180 Roberts	☐ 207 Windham
☐ 126 St. George	☐ 154 Beckman	☐ 181 Terrill	

$1.95 each

☐ 208 Halston	☐ 212 Young	☐ 216 Saunders	☐ 220 Hampson
☐ 209 LaDame	☐ 213 Dailey	☐ 217 Vitek	☐ 221 Browning
☐ 210 Eden	☐ 214 Hampson	☐ 218 Hunter	☐ 222 Carroll
☐ 211 Walters	☐ 215 Roberts	☐ 219 Cork	☐ 223 Summers

IT'S YOUR OWN SPECIAL TIME

Contemporary romances for today's women.
Each month, six very special love stories will be yours
from SILHOUETTE. Look for them wherever books are sold
or order now from the coupon below.

$1.95 each

☐ 224 Langan	☐ 243 Saunders	☐ 262 John	☐ 281 Lovan
☐ 225 St. George	☐ 244 Sinclair	☐ 263 Wilson	☐ 282 Halldorson
☐ 226 Hamson	☐ 245 Trent	☐ 264 Vine	☐ 283 Payne
☐ 227 Beckman	☐ 246 Carroll	☐ 265 Adams	☐ 284 Young
☐ 228 King	☐ 247 Halldorson	☐ 266 Trent	☐ 285 Gray
☐ 229 Thornton	☐ 248 St. George	☐ 267 Chase	☐ 286 Cork
☐ 230 Stevens	☐ 249 Scofield	☐ 268 Hunter	☐ 287 Joyce
☐ 231 Dailey	☐ 250 Hampson	☐ 269 Smith	☐ 288 Smith
☐ 232 Hampson	☐ 251 Wilson	☐ 270 Camp	☐ 289 Saunders
☐ 233 Vernon	☐ 252 Roberts	☐ 271 Allison	☐ 290 Hunter
☐ 234 Smith	☐ 253 James	☐ 272 Forrest	☐ 291 McKay
☐ 235 James	☐ 254 Palmer	☐ 273 Beckman	☐ 292 Browning
☐ 236 Maxam	☐ 255 Smith	☐ 274 Roberts	☐ 293 Morgan
☐ 237 Wilson	☐ 256 Hampson	☐ 275 Browning	☐ 294 Cockcroft
☐ 238 Cork	☐ 257 Hunter	☐ 276 Vernon	☐ 295 Vernon
☐ 239 McKay	☐ 258 Ashby	☐ 277 Wilson	☐ 296 Paige
☐ 240 Hunter	☐ 259 English	☐ 278 Hunter	☐ 297 Young
☐ 241 Wisdom	☐ 260 Martin	☐ 279 Ashby	
☐ 242 Brooke	☐ 261 Saunders	☐ 280 Roberts	

SILHOUETTE BOOKS, Department SB/1

1230 Avenue of the Americas
New York, NY 10020

Please send me the books I have checked above. I am enclosing $_____
(please add 75¢ to cover postage and handling. NYS and NYC residents please
add appropriate sales tax). Send check or money order—no cash or C.O.D.'s
please. Allow six weeks for delivery.

NAME _____

ADDRESS _____

CITY _____ STATE/ZIP _____

Silhouette Romance

Coming Next Month

Song of Surrender by Elizabeth Hunter

A tempermental and exacting taskmaster, David Lloyd wanted Katy as his pupil. Katy knew this would advance her singing career, but could she resist the sweet insistence of his lovemaking?

Less of A Stranger by Nora Roberts

Megan and David clashed over his plans for the amusement park she ran. But Megan wanted the restless, roaming David, and at Joyland, dreams were supposed to come true.

The Felstead Collection by Kay Stephens

Jay was hired to determine whether the paintings in the priceless Felstead collection were real. But soon she was wondering if the love of dark, enigmatic Rhys Felstead was a true one.

Roomful of Roses by Diana Palmer

Only one thing stood in the way of Wynn's marriage—her legal guardian, McCabe Foxe. The tough war correspondent invaded her life again—and lay siege to her heart.

Best of Enemies by Joan Smith

Toni Ewell and Jack Beldon drew battle lines over the planned demolition of a town landmark. But sometimes the best of enemies can turn into something more than friends.

No Gentle Love by Ruth Langan

It took a man like Drew Carlson to recognize the sensuality beneath Kate Halloran's tailored suit. He hoped she'd find a love that wasn't forecast in the annual reports.